PRACTICAL
MEMORY

Isaac Robledo is an internationally bestselling author who received his B.A. from Purdue University in psychology, and his M.S. from the University of Oklahoma in industrial-organizational psychology. His books are meant to help readers build their intellectual, creative, and mindful abilities.

PRACTICAL MEMORY

A Simple Guide to Help You Remember More
and Forget Less in Your Everyday Life

Isaac Robledo

RUPA

Published by
Rupa Publications India Pvt. Ltd 2022
7/16, Ansari Road, Daryaganj
New Delhi 110002

Sales Centres:
Allahabad Bengaluru Chennai
Hyderabad Jaipur Kathmandu
Kolkata Mumbai

Copyright © Isaac Robledo 2022

The views and opinions expressed in this book are the author's own and the facts are as reported by him which have been verified to the extent possible, and the publishers are not in any way liable for the same.

All rights reserved.
No part of this publication may be reproduced, transmitted, or stored in a retrieval system, in any form or by any means, electronic, mechanical, photocopying, recording or otherwise, without the prior permission of the publisher.

ISBN: 978-93-5520-831-6

First impression 2022

10 9 8 7 6 5 4 3 2 1

Printed in India

This book is sold subject to the condition that it shall not, by way of trade or otherwise, be lent, resold, hired out, or otherwise circulated, without the publisher's prior consent, in any form of binding or cover other than that in which it is published.

CONTENTS

An Introduction to Practical Memory	7
Before You Continue…	16
The Most Common Memory Failures	17
Practice Your Memory	36
Build New Memories	49
Recover "Lost" Memories	81
Externalize Memories	100
Geographical & Travel Memories	113
Concluding Thoughts	133
Isaac Robledo's Thoughts	141
Thank You	142
Did You Learn Something New?	143
More Books by Isaac Robledo	144

AN INTRODUCTION TO PRACTICAL MEMORY

"In a sense, he thought, all we consist of is memories. Our personalities are constructed from memories, our lives are organized around memories, and our cultures are built upon the foundation of shared memories that we call history and science."

—Norman, from *The Sphere*, a novel by Michael Crichton

Does the World Need Another Memory Book?

You might have noticed that there are many other books available to help you with your memory. Some of them are from memory experts or champions of memory competitions. So the question is, why would you need another memory book? Haven't the ones out there said everything there is to say on the topic?

Well, what is missing are tips on how we can improve our memory in a *practical way*, for the things that most of us need to remember on a regular basis.

This book will probably not help you to win a memory championship or perform amazing feats of memory that will impress your friends. But what it will help you with is the memory issues that you experience in your normal life.

Many of the most common memory complaints are not actually addressed in other memory books, whereas they are directly tackled here. Some of these include forgetting where you parked the car, the reason why you entered a room, where you left the keys or your wallet, or losing your train of thought, and so forth. All of these situations and much more will be covered herein.

Who is This Book for?

This book is for you, if you are worried that your memory may be getting worse, and you want a practical resource that can help you begin improving your ability to remember right now.

Perhaps you are not interested in spending much of your time learning very elaborate memory techniques. Instead, you would like to learn simple strategies quickly that you can begin to apply right away in your life. If so, you will find this book highly useful.

Another reason to continue reading is if you would like to strengthen any weak areas in your memory. Some of us are naturally good at remembering numbers, but not so good with faces. Or you may be good with remembering places and navigating, but not at remembering items on a grocery list. Regardless, this book can be a great resource for improving in weak areas which have given you trouble.

What Does it Mean to Have a Practical Memory?

I think we all have an understanding of what "practical" means. The more life experience I acquire, the more I tend to value practical approaches. This means taking an approach of looking for efficient actions you can take that actually get the results you are looking for. And the results most of us are looking for are the ones that help us in our everyday lives. We are *not* looking for advice that is overly difficult to apply, or that only applies to very few people in rare circumstances.

The *Practical Memory* approach is to keep things simple. Why make things complicated with systems that take longer to learn than what you are actually trying to remember? This approach means focusing your memory on the most important areas of your life that you truly need to know. This also means knowing what *not* to remember. Contrary to what some may think, the goal should not be to remember everything. Information that is not important, or that can easily be recorded in some other way does not necessarily need to be memorized. With the practical approach, we realize that memory is a tool, and one that can be sharpened to help you remember in a more sensible way.

Something you will *not* find here is theoretical discussions on the nature of memory itself. Memory is an interesting topic, but if you want to learn more about types of memory, how it works, or the biological nature of memory, you could find better sources for this elsewhere. Although I believe the field is interesting and I would welcome you to learn more about it, this book will instead focus on helping you to improve your memory. Rather than going into detail about *why* these memory tips work, I will simply present them to you so you can apply them and see the benefits of using them immediately.

If the point here is to have a practical approach to building a better memory, then where should these tips come from? From memory experts? That could make sense, but in my experience, because they are experts and have spent years learning and applying detailed and complicated systems, it is easy to get lost and feel overwhelmed if you are new to their complex ways of memorizing.

The analogy I would use is that you might feel completely overwhelmed if you are new to martial arts, and you train with a martial arts guru who wishes to teach you super-sophisticated techniques. Actually, a beginner would probably get a much better start by taking a much simpler but highly effective self-defense course. Such a course would focus more on what you really need to know, rather than overwhelming you with complicated techniques. This book is like that self-defense course, showing you the most important things you must know to develop a better memory, *instead* of overwhelming you.

Memory doesn't actually have to be very complicated. Since I was young I've had a deep interest in the mind, intelligence, and of course memory, and how we can improve ourselves in this regard. I've always paid close attention when someone made an off-hand comment about a tip or trick they used to remember things. Often, I find that the types of tips people use in their real lives are much better and more reliable than those I've heard of from experts in memory. In time, I realized that these memory tips from real people with great memories should all be compiled into a single place. That is the aim of this book. Often, these tips are simple and easy to apply, and of course effective, which is what makes them practical.

In your course of reading, you may think some of the tips included are obvious or "common sense". I like what Voltaire said though. He said:

"Common sense is not so common."

Many of the tips, although you may think they should be obvious, will be new to many readers. It is easy to make the mistake of going through life without learning these memory tips, and to possibly make remembering much more difficult than it has to be. This book is meant to help make things a bit easier for you. If you were already aware of a tip, then great! But remember that many people had overlooked it, and learning it should improve their ability to remember from here on.

My Story with Memory

Many years ago, I had just started a graduate program. After a few weeks, I started to notice that I was having major memory issues. My problem was bad enough that I had a lot of trouble forming new memories, or learning. I frequently had to ask someone to repeat things for me, or I had to look at my notes over and over since I couldn't remember what was said in the meetings I had attended. This was the first time I ever had such an issue. I was worried enough about it that I made a doctor's appointment.

When I went to the doctor, and he asked me many questions, I realized that there were multiple issues going on at once.

1. **Attention problem**
   Really, at the core of my memory problem, it seemed like I had a lot of trouble paying attention. I couldn't seem to keep my focus at all.
2. **Sleeping problem**
   I had a great deal of work which overwhelmed me, and I couldn't sleep. Often, I would only get about two hours of sleep a night, and I didn't have time to take any naps in the day.
3. **Eating habits problem**
   I tended to skip breakfast, or sometimes eat a yogurt, and I didn't have much of an appetite, so I was eating much less than I should have in general.

4. **Stress problem**
I was living in a new state, without friends or family in the area. Also, I had more work to do than I had ever had before, and I was expected to learn many things quite fast. The pressure to perform gave me excessive stress.

My doctor's visit made me realize that my memory was bad, but there were a lot of other factors that probably caused this. My high stress levels led to poor sleeping and poor eating habits. It also led to a poor ability to pay attention. If I wasn't paying attention, then I wouldn't remember. My point here is that your memory can be affected by many other areas of your life. If your memory isn't as good as you would like, consider some other key areas – your attention, sleep, eating & nutrition, and stress levels.

To offer a bit more support than just my personal story, consider that Dr. Fabiny in the Harvard Health article *Tips to get the most from your memory* has stated something similar: "Get enough sleep, reduce stress, and check with your doctor to see if any of your medications affect memory — all three are potential memory spoilers."

To wrap up my story, the doctor prescribed medicine to help me sleep, and I also had to learn to manage the stress. Talking it out, meditation, and breathing exercises helped with this. It took some time, but with constant effort on improving, my memory did improve until finally it was back to its normal state. At this point, many years have passed and I've been able to further improve my memory, with tips such as the ones you will soon discover here.

The reason I mention my story with memory early on is because you need to be sure to have these areas of your life in order first. If you have poor attention, sleeping, nutrition, and stress, then it is quite likely that you will have memory issues.

Did You Really Forget?

People often say, "I don't remember", in response to questions, but usually this isn't quite accurate.

When you forget something from here on, I want you to ask yourself "Did I really forget it?" Chances are something else is at work here, not just your memory.

In my story above, the direct problem that affected my memory was actually my inattention, which was caused by stress, lack of sleep, and bad nutrition.

If you lack attention when you are taking in information, this means you aren't forming a clear picture of what you wanted to remember. But of course, it is important for you to develop this clear picture, so that you can then recall it later on. Otherwise, it is like trying to recall details by looking at a fuzzy image. If you often lose your focus and attention, you will need to overcome this before your memory begins to improve.

You also need intention if you wish to remember. We are bombarded with so much information every day that it can be overwhelming. Therefore, you must *intend* to remember something, if you are ever going to actually remember it. If nothing seems especially important or eventful to you, and you have no intentions to remember, then you won't. You will forget, and forget fast.

You also need to get organized, which will help you to build an understanding. We are not computers. Computers can remember (or at least record) everything with no understanding of it. People need to have some understanding of the information, otherwise it seems like nonsense and becomes impossible to remember. Organizing information helps you to understand it and make it meaningful, which helps you to remember it.

I want to tell a quick story to show you the importance of *understanding* to memory. When I was in elementary school I was once given a test where I was asked to remember a series of nonsense syllables. This means they were word-like bits that made no sense, such as "om", "sem", "tog", etc. I was worried because as soon as I was given the test, I realized I could not remember any of these "words". The reason? There was no way to understand these nonsense words. Since it was gibberish to me, the words escaped my mind almost as fast as they entered it.

The point here is simple. Understanding is key to building memories. Some people plan to memorize everything, and don't care whether they understand or not. If you do so, you are making the process of learning much harder than it needs to be.

Have you ever wondered why adults do not remember their early childhood years? I believe a big part of the reason is that children lack a fundamental understanding of the world, and therefore lack strong memories. I think those early years are meant to give children a basic understanding, so they can begin to develop memories. Of course, learning your first language is a key tool for understanding.

The bottom line here is simple. Keep your attention, intention, organization, and understanding in mind before you blame a poor memory. Your memory may not be as bad as you think.

Introducing the Main Goals of *Practical Memory*

This is a very brief overview of what exactly you will be learning in *Practical Memory*.

1. **Common Memory Failures**
   We will look at some of the most common everyday

memory issues that people have, and how to deal with them.

2. **Practice Your Memory**
Tips for how to practice improving your general memory abilities.

3. **Build New Memories**
Learn how to build new memories in the areas most important to you.

4. **Recover "Lost" Memories**
When you just can't seem to remember something, here are some tips to help recover those memories that you seem to have lost.

5. **Externalize Memories**
Why, how, and when you should use outside devices or sources to help you remember.

6. **Geographical & Travel Memories**
Tips to remember directions, travel routes, and stop getting lost.

Please note that this book can be read in any order, depending on your needs. If only certain sections appeal to you, you may skip directly to them. Because of this, a few parts have some repetition, but that is to make sure that each section tells you everything you need to know on its own. If you read the book from beginning to end, keep in mind that this repetition isn't necessarily bad. It may also be helpful because you will find that the parts which are discussed more than once are probably more important and worth remembering.

BEFORE YOU CONTINUE...

As a thank you for reading, I want you to have this free guide:

Step Up Your Learning: Free Tools to Learn Almost Anything

Have you ever wondered what the best sites and resources for learning are? It takes time and effort to figure out which sites are worth it and which are not. I hope to save you some of that time so you can spend more of it learning instead of searching the Internet.

In the past ten years or so, there has been a free learning revolution happening. More and more resources for learning are becoming available to the public at no cost. With so many new ones coming out, it's easy to miss out on some of the great learning opportunities available. Fortunately for you, this guide is short at around 4,000 words, and tells you exactly what you need to know.

The guide stems from my own experiences of using a variety of learning sites and resources. In it, you will discover the best places to go for learning at no cost. Also, I'll explain which resources are best for you, depending on your learning goals.

You can download this free guide as a PDF by clicking here or by typing this website into your browser: http://mentalmax.net/EN

Now, let's get back on topic.

THE MOST COMMON MEMORY FAILURES

A Brief Introduction

I often hear about certain memory complaints: forgetting a name, where the car was parked, or where you left something that you use every day. I am sure you have seen this in others or experienced it yourself. These common memory failures have sometimes been described as "senior moments", which is when you have trouble recalling something that you should know or remember. Because of the name, you may think these would happen more often in older people. However, a Trending Machine national poll of 800 adults found that such senior moments are now *more common* in young people than in actual seniors.

According to the poll, millennials (age 18-34) were significantly more likely than seniors aged 55+ to forget what day it is (15% vs. 7%), where they had left the keys (14% vs. 8%), to forget their lunch (9% vs. 3%), or to bathe (6% vs. 2%). The only thing seniors were *significantly* more likely to forget, was a name (23% vs. 16%).

Given such data, we have to be careful about assuming that memory issues are something that only happens to older people. One reason younger people may have memory issues is that we now rely less on our memories, as we tend to go to our smartphones and computers to store or search for information, rather than to recall it ourselves. Using your memory is important, as it will become stronger through exercising it, and weaker through lack of use.

In this section, we will explore common memory complaints that have been seen across age groups and in a wide variety of people. Don't assume that smart people are immune from such memory lapses, as I have personally seen many of them suffer from them just as often as anyone else. The truth is we all experience such memory lapses from time to time, and so we should learn how to deal with these issues first.

Where Did I Park the Car?

In *Moonwalking with Einstein*, by Joshua Foer, the author is seemingly a normal person who underwent special memory training, and went on to win the USA Memory Championship in 2006. This was surprising because his competition was a group of people who seemed to have supernatural memories. Although, in reality it turned out that all of his competition had built up their memories through rigorous training as well. His competitors had likely trained for years, whereas Joshua trained only for about one year, under the guidance of British Grand Master of Memory, Ed Cooke.

At the end of the book, Foer comically reveals that even after winning this memory competition, he had forgotten where he parked the car. Some people who read the book may have felt that learning how to improve memory is useless if you can win a competition and still forget where you parked the car. But really, this just proves how important attention and intention are. You must pay attention, and you must intend to remember, or you will likely forget. Joshua Foer has simply demonstrated that just because you are excellent at remembering certain things (such as the order of a deck of cards), doesn't mean you will remember everything.

Many of us have cars, and we usually remember where we parked them, but there are few things more annoying than forgetting where you left one of your most valuable assets. Now, let's cover some tips on how to avoid this problem from here on.

Look Back

You will want to process where you left the car from a different angle, such as looking back at it after you've walked several steps away, as this will show it to you from another perspective. When you look back, you should pay attention to whether there is anything near your car that stands out. Don't pay much attention to surrounding cars, because they are likely to move before you return.

The funny thing is that many of us will park the car, and our minds will wander toward what we are about to do. Perhaps we are shopping, or exploring a new area, or something else. We are in a rush to move forward, and so it doesn't occur to us to simply look back and see the car from another angle.

Unfortunately, this means that the only time you will actually see the car is when you parked it. As you leave, you are no longer looking at the vehicle. Because of this, it is difficult to build a complete mental picture of where you actually parked it. Of course, the important thing you need to know when looking for your car is the path to get back to the vehicle, not the path that you took to leave it. Simply looking back is a way to help fix this.

Remember the row

If you forget everything about where you left your car, try to remember this. Remember the row or aisle where you parked it. As we all know, usually parking areas are just a boring pattern of repeating cars, so it can be difficult to find anything distinctive to remember exactly where you parked. For that reason, I recommend focusing on the ends of the rows. One end will often lead to where you are going, such as a shop. The other end may lead away to somewhere else, perhaps nothing, but maybe a restaurant or other shop. Observe what is at the ends of the row your car is on, and try to remember that.

If you know the row, you should be able to find the car. This is because usually we have at least a rough idea of the distance down the row where we parked. Since we already walked down it once, we tend to remember walking that distance. The problem is we often forget the row, because they mostly look alike. Make an effort to remember the row, and what is on the ends of them, because this is one of the few features you can use to help you remember where you left your vehicle. I'm sure we've all had the experience of being off by even one row, which can be aggravating because it is usually difficult to see your car even at this distance, with many cars blocking the view.

Take a snapshot

Another option is to take a picture of the parking section you are in, or text it to yourself. If you are in a massive parking garage or a massive lot with all kinds of rows and numberings, possibly with multiple floors, this may not be the time to test your memory. If you do, the risk is that you won't be able to find your car at all. These tend to be the types of places that you may be leaving your vehicle at for a longer time, such as an airport or a large shopping center. Of course, the problem is that the longer you are away, the more likely it is that you will forget where you parked. For these reasons, I simply recommend recording exactly where you left the car. Note the floor, the row, the section, any numbers, etc. You can text it to yourself or take a picture. If your phone battery is low, also be sure to send the information to someone else, preferably a companion that you are with (or they can record it themselves). As a side tip, you might put your phone on "low power" mode to conserve battery life.

What was the Name Again?

Forgetting someone's name is a pretty common memory problem. It's even worse when we have just met the person. But the best time to focus on remembering someone's name actually is right after meeting them. These are tips that will help when you have been introduced to someone new.

Do you know someone else with the same name?

When you meet someone new, it can help to remember anyone else you know with the same name and associate them together in some way. Do they remind you of each other? Are they similar in appearance, age, profession, or in any way at all? Even if they are opposites, thinking about how opposite they are to each other might help you to remember the name later on. Actually, the mere act of trying to remember other people with similar names can help strengthen your memory of this person.

What does the name remind you of?

When you learn a new name that isn't very familiar, or perhaps you don't personally know anyone with the name, then it can help to think of what else the name makes you think of. For example, what if you meet someone called Monty, and you don't know anyone else with that name? What does it make you think of? To me, Monty resembles the word mount, or mountain. To help remember Monty's name, you could visualize him wearing a hat that looks like a mountain. If it helps, you might even bring mountains into the conversation. You could ask him if he grew up near any mountains, for example. Making these types of associations will help you recall the name later on.

Say it aloud

Say the name out loud, as soon as you can. When the person says their name, repeat it back to them. Sometimes people speak fast, so if you didn't get it, then ask them to repeat it. This repetition of the name will help you to remember it later. For the more unusual names that you may not have heard before, this will be a more important step. If necessary, also ask the spelling if that will help you to nail it down and remember it later. Don't think that you are bothering the person, because they will probably appreciate that someone wants to make sure to remember their name.

Recall names in their presence

If you have just met many different people, spend a bit of time looking around to practice recalling their names while they are still around. You want to keep these names active in your mind. If you just learned many different names, it may be easy to forget them if you don't keep them in your mind a bit longer. To do this, perhaps you could have a polite conversation about one of these new people with someone else you know. Of course, this gives you another chance to say their name out loud and practice recalling it. And if you forget a name, you can simply ask the host or someone else to help remind you. It will be easier to form new memories while still in the presence of these people you have just met. Later on when you get home, the names may already be forgotten if you haven't made a special effort to recall them.

Where did I Put the Keys? (Or phone, or purse / wallet, etc.)

This is all too common. How much time has humanity lost searching for items that we ourselves put down somewhere? It's easy to do, because often the mind is somewhere else, or we are distracted and we put things down wherever they fall, mindlessly. Luckily, here are some tips to help put a stop to this pattern of forgetting where we put our possessions.

Be mindful and present

Bear with me if you don't like this option, but one simple way to remember where you left something is to be mindful and present, which is to pay attention to what you are doing. We forget where we left the keys because our minds are in what we are eating for dinner, what work still needs to get done before tomorrow, and the phone that is ringing that we need to pick up. It's much easier said than done, but actually thinking about what we are doing, instead of loads of other things, will take us a long way in remembering.

This technique can take some training or self-discipline, but to put extra thought in these little everyday actions can help us remember them better. If you think of it, much of our lives are made up of these little everyday actions. If we are not mindful during them, it is easy to run through much of our lives on autopilot, not processing much of what we are doing, which then results in not remembering much of what we have done.

Leave items in the same place

Alternatively, you may not truly need to remember where you left your items. If you have one place where you always leave the keys and any other common forgotten items you have, then you no longer need to burden your memory with this. If you are often distracted or multi-tasking, and you can't realistically expect yourself to be mindful and pay attention to what you are doing, then leaving your items in the same place every day could be the best choice. This "same place" can be whatever works for you. It may be a basket, a place on your desk where you only place these items and nothing else, or anywhere that is convenient. The downside of this strategy is that it will not exercise your memory, but you can be pretty sure that you will stop losing your items.

What if you just can't find it?

I'd like to include a few quick tips, in case you actually did lose something, and you can't remember where you left it. First, try retracing your steps. What rooms have you gone into? Could it be in the garage, in a shed, in the basement, your vehicle, etc.? Also, remember to search the last pair of pants or jacket or any clothing you were wearing that might have had pockets. It's possible that some of those clothes would be in the laundry basket by now. If your office or room is cluttered, be sure to check underneath clothing or anything else lying around – as something may be on top of what you are looking for. Also, sometimes objects can fall in between the cushions of a couch, or fall underneath something, such as your bed, where your eyes can't easily see what is there unless you specifically look. Keep in mind that if you repeatedly can't find your smartphone, there are apps you can use to help track it.

What Did I Come Here for Again?

You enter a room and you have no idea why. You're pretty sure you came for a reason, to find something, to do something, but what could it be? Here are some tips to help you figure out such mysteries.

Mentally retrace your steps

To exercise your ability to remember, the best way to handle these situations is to mentally retrace what you were doing. If you find this to be difficult, and you just can't remember anything, push through that and search. The more difficult this is for you, the more of a sign it is that you need to push yourself to remember. By exercising this ability, you can help improve it.

When this does happen, flip the question from "What did I come here for" to "What was I just doing?" What you were just doing will often provide the biggest clue as to what you were about to do. If you ask yourself questions about what you were doing, this should help to remind you what you were thinking and what you were trying to achieve. Then you will remember why you entered the room.

Return to the scene of the cue

If you are looking for an easier way to resolve this problem, or if you simply had too much trouble remembering, then there is another way. Go back to what you were doing before you entered this new room. Often, something that you were doing will have triggered you to go to the new room to look for something, or to do something. For example, if you were in your office, go back there, and return to what you were doing. If you were on the computer, check what you were looking at on the screen. Perhaps when you view the computer screen, you see a recipe for a dish you wanted to cook. Then you remember that you went to the kitchen because you wanted to check if you had all of the ingredients to make a specific recipe. Things aren't always this simple, but sometimes it is as simple as a word or picture you saw. Anything could have triggered you to go to another room. Look for those triggers, and you will figure it out.

Tip of the Tongue Problem

The "Tip of the tongue" problem is what happens when you know that you know something, and you feel that you are almost able to remember it and say it, but you just can't quite get it out. Maybe you have an idea of what the word starts with, or you can visualize a face but not the name. Either way, this is frustrating, because you almost have it, and you feel so close, but you just can't recall it completely.

Break the loop

It's easy to find yourself in a thought loop, where you keep going back to the same frustrating thought. For example, perhaps you can make out that it starts with a "P", so maybe you keep making the "P" sound, but repeating such patterns in your mind over and over won't get you anywhere. This isn't an effective way to rebuild a memory. All it does is add to the frustration. How do you break the loop? With the following tips.

Search for associations

Search for any associated memories with the thing that you want to remember. This may involve related people, countries, foods, objects, music, names, etc. Everything that you come up with will be a clue to help you remember the actual item you are trying to remember. For example, if you are trying to remember the name of a band, it can help to recall their songs, replaying them in your mind and thinking of the song lyrics. You might recall interviews they've done, or even what type of clothes they wear. Bringing to mind all kinds of associations with the band will make it much more likely that you actually remember the name.

Think of letters and sounds

Often when I am trying to remember something, and it is on the tip of my tongue, I get an idea of sounds or letters that are in the name of what I want to remember, although I won't see the complete picture. In my experience, my instincts are often right, and it helps to give me a starting point to remember.

I have a convenient example. The other day, I was trying to remember an actor's name from *The Fast and the Furious* movie series. It was on the tip of my tongue, and I had the letter V in mind, but I wasn't sure if this was a part of the first or last name. I decided to start thinking through any possible names that could start with V. I got to the answer fairly quickly, because first I thought Vance, then Vince, but when I thought of Vince, it sounded right, but not quite. So I realized that it was Vin, not Vince, then that was enough to make me remember it was Vin Diesel. So keep in mind that you don't necessarily need to remember the full name immediately. Often, if you get close, it will help you obtain the full memory.

Recover "Lost" memories

Really, this problem of wanting to remember things that seem to have slipped away from us is common enough that I have dedicated another section of the book to it. These tips will definitely help you get started when you have something on the tip of your tongue, but for other times when you are frustrated and can't recall a memory, even though you feel you should know it, the section Recover "Lost" Memories will help you even more.

What was that Address, Phone Number, or Birth Date? (And other such numbers & details)

It seems very common now that people rarely remember numbers. I don't think this is because we have such a bad memory for numbers, but because we rely more and more on technology to remember them for us.

People used to (and I'm sure some still do) keep address or phone books of their own to record the numbers of important people in their lives. And they were more likely to remember some of these numbers because they knew they would actually have to dial them out by hand every time they wanted to call. Now, most people keep these numbers logged in their smartphones. This means if you want to dial someone, you just find their name and press the button. You don't actually have to press any numbers. So of course, we don't tend to remember numbers, since we don't pay attention to them to begin with.

Go back to the old way of recording

A simple fix for this forgetfulness of numbers is to go back to writing down the numbers in your life that you want to remember. These are numbers that are important to you, that you should probably know by heart.

Imagine if your car broke down on a road trip, and your phone was dead (with all the recorded numbers of people you know). Think of how silly it would look if this happened, and someone stopped to help you and they offered you their phone. Then, you would realize that you can't remember anyone's phone number. As unlikely as it may seem, phone batteries die all the time, and even new cars can break down.

I recommend writing down all types of numbers and other details that you would like to remember. This can include addresses, phone numbers, birth dates, identification numbers (although if these are sensitive, be sure to keep them protected). Keep a running list. It doesn't need to be very big. It could include immediate family members, close friends, and perhaps a doctor or other important person in your life.

Don't overwhelm yourself. Start off with the five most important numbers and details you need to learn. When you remember those, then do the next five, and so on.

Of course, you have to realize that just writing them down will not be enough to force you to memorize them. Be sure to review these numbers occasionally to make sure you actually know them. If you do not review, you will tend to forget them with time.

A good way to test yourself will be to actually dial the numbers out the old fashioned way on your phone. It takes longer, but you will be sure you are remembering them correctly. Or you could test yourself by writing down the numbers from memory, then checking if you did so correctly. You may review them once a day for a few days, then once a week, then once a month, until you are sure you have memorized them.

Seeing patterns in the numbers

Numbers don't have much meaning for us generally, so they can be more difficult to remember. A simple way to help you remember numbers in general is to see patterns in them. You may notice whether a phone number (or other number) is mostly odd digits or even. Are the numbers going up in order, or down in order more often? Try to think if you have seen some groupings of these numbers somewhere else. Are some numbers your age, or the age of someone you know? Are they the year of someone's birth? Are they the jersey number of a player in a sport you follow? Are they the height or weight of someone you know? Another way to look at it is in terms of mathematical patterns. For the number 248, you might notice that each number is double the prior one. You could look for any other such patterns, perhaps involving addition, subtraction, or division. By seeing patterns such as this, it will be much easier for you to remember the digits since they will hold some kind of meaning for you.

Use idle time

This is meant to be a practical book, and realistically I can see that most of us don't want to spend time remembering numbers. It's kind of boring, right? What I do, and what I would recommend is that when you are sitting around waiting at the doctor's office, or waiting for anything, to spend a few minutes and quiz yourself on phone numbers in your phone. A lot of modern time is spent waiting, so we might as well train our memory skills during some of that time.

I Lost My Train of Thought

You're having a conversation with someone, and you've set up your point perfectly. You're just about to make your point, and you realize you forgot what it was. You forgot where you were going with what you were saying.

Some people, like myself, tend to get ideas upon ideas in the course of normal conversations. Anything someone says might spark many different directions for me to think about. This may involve interesting things I've read or seen lately. Sometimes though, what pops into my mind doesn't actually have much to do with the main topic. Or if it does, it takes quite a bit of background explanation to finally show that there is indeed a connection between this new topic in my mind and the topic already being discussed. These tendencies can make it more likely to lose your train of thought.

Losing your train of thought is common enough. I've seen it in all types of people, and in all age groups. The following are tips to help make it so you don't forget what you wanted to say.

Keep track of the main topics

Get used to keeping track of the themes you are discussing. Often, during conversation you are talking about specific details of events, but remember what the overall idea is of what you are talking about. For example, it may be relationship problems, how children should be disciplined, or your favorite movies. Try to keep track of these topics, and be mindful as they shift from one to the other.

Ideas can become connected so fluidly that it's easy to lose track of what the original topic was. For example, a conversation about your favorite movie, if it is *Interstellar*, may drift to talking about how the company SpaceX plans to go to Mars. This makes you think of your childhood dream to become an astronaut, which leads you to think of how your father didn't like the idea of his kids traveling to outer space, which turns you to the arguments your parents used to have that led to their divorce. Where did I start this mess with? See how easy it is to get lost? In reality, conversations won't always shift topics that fast, but it does happen. Keep those main topics in mind on a large overview level, and it will be easier to keep your train of thought.

Distractions in the environment can also make you forget what you were thinking about. For example, if there is a dramatic unexpected interruption, such as a child running around and falling and hurting himself, then crying loudly, this sort of thing can jolt you out of where your mind was. If you were keeping track of topics, however, it will be easier to find your place where you left off.

Going off on a tangent

If at any point you are going off on a tangent–to discuss something not so related to your original topic, make an extra effort to hold on to the original topic, or the original point that you left off from. That original topic is like your home, and you have chosen to wander off into the woods, but you need to remember the way back. This is because if you are going on a tangent, you are still expected in conversation to somehow tie it back in to the original topic. And also, when moving on to other topics, it is easy to forget where you started. Making this extra effort should help. It can take practice, but if you like to wander off in different directions in your conversations, you will want to keep track of your key themes.

Oh No! I Left my Wallet / Purse, Phone Charger, Souvenir, Wedding Ring, etc.

My father is a smart person, but as I have stated, smart people are not exempt from memory lapses. He has been known to lose many expensive cameras he's owned in places such as taxi cabs, hotels, and so forth. He is a busy businessperson, so often when something like this happens, he has simply cut his losses and moved on.

The only way to really save these cameras for him would have been to have some sort of a system to make sure he would not forget them. We can't save those lost cameras, but there is still hope to help you avoid losing precious items of your own.

Always know the number of bags or suitcases you have with you

If you make note of the number of bags you have with you, then this will help make it so you are less likely to forget any of them. Clearly, if you enter an area with three bags, then you should leave with those three bags. This is just a basic way to check that you are not forgetting anything that you were carrying with you.

Do a final check of your area before you leave

I have traveled quite often in the past few years. One thing I've noticed is that it isn't just my father who has the problem of leaving items behind, even valuable ones. For example, on a recent trip to an airport, I found a passport that had been left at the security checkpoint area. I gave it to the security personnel. A few steps later as I was leaving the security area, I saw someone's driver's license on a chair, with no one nearby. These are pretty important items to leave behind, and I would like to help prevent you from forgetting items like these or other valuables.

Unfortunately, it is very easy to forget things when we are moving around. The simple way to avoid this issue is to look back at the area you are leaving, before you go. Whether you are getting ready to leave a bus, hotel room, or a restaurant, etc., before you leave you can simply look back at your area to make sure you did not forget anything.

It seems a bit silly, but every time I am going to leave a hotel, I check the drawers, electric sockets, under the bed, etc., to make sure I am not leaving anything behind. If you adopt such a system, you will no longer need to worry about forgetting something valuable.

Put the things you might forget and the things you would never forget, in the same place

When you are traveling, or in a place outside of your home, make a note of anything important you could possibly forget. These are things like jewelry, a camera, your wallet, etc. Then, you are likely to have other items you could not possibly forget. This might be something like your car keys (you need them to drive away), your suitcase, or your coat (assuming it is cold).

The advice here is simple. Take those possessions you feel that you *might* forget, and assume that you *will* forget them. We all tend to assume the best, and that everything will be fine. But for now, just assume anything that you might forget, you will, and that your job is to prevent that from happening. Then, take any of these items that you might forget and put them directly on, or directly next to the items you could not possibly forget.

For example, if someone gave you a gift bag of exotic chocolates, this is something you might forget. What you could do if you are traveling, is put it in your luggage, or on it, or right to the side of it. This way, when you are in a rush later on and ready to go because the taxi has arrived, you won't forget the chocolates.

If you have lost items in the past, I highly recommend using a system like this. Just remember to put the items you would not forget, and the items you could forget right next to each other. However, be aware that if they are even a foot away from each other, you still might forget something if you are in a rush.

PRACTICE YOUR MEMORY

A Brief Introduction

An important reason you are probably reading this book is to generally improve your memory abilities. Like with anything else, the way to do this is through practice. Through repeatedly exercising your memory, you will strengthen your ability to remember new information.

What this means is you will want to create situations to practice your memory. If some of the practice exercises given are too difficult, then you will know you have found a weakness in your memory. This will be something you will want to spend *more* time practicing, so that you can improve your ability. If you struggle at first, this is normal. With more practice, it will get easier. However, if you avoid practice, your weak areas will only continue to be weak.

After an Event, Practice Remembering it

Perhaps you have just gotten through a phone call, maybe you attended a lecture, watched a movie, or read a book. For anything you have just done or experienced, an easy way to practice building up your memory is to simply remember the event. This practice will be a great habit for you to build up your ability to remember.

Often, it takes some time and deliberation to work through

a thought and to fully process it. If you are constantly moving from one task or activity to the next and to the next, without time to think through anything that has just happened, your memories will be more likely to suffer because of it.

Instead, after you have done something important that you know you want to remember again later, practice remembering soon thereafter. This will help you to be able to recall it in greater detail at a later time.

If you think of it, practicing remembering is really just a way of testing yourself.

The following can apply for anyone, but if you are a student you may be especially interested. Let's discuss a very thorough investigation by John Dunlosky and other researchers, titled "Improving Students Learning with Effective Learning Techniques", in *Psychological Science in the Public Interest*. These researchers examined hundreds of articles and looked for which learning techniques had the most scientific support. Ultimately, they found that self-testing was one of the best ways to learn and remember. They also found that an *ineffective* strategy students often use is to simply read their notes, over and over. The better option is actually to test yourself, as this helps you to see what areas you are strong in, and what areas you are weak in. That way, you can spend more time on those weak areas, and you do not need to waste time reviewing areas you are quite strong in.

Testing yourself is quite simple. You would just make up a test for yourself. You can do this by making up a test for the items you want to learn. Or, you can simply ask yourself questions mentally or verbally, and seek your own answers. For example, you may check if you can remember definitions and other important facts from a history book. The key point of this system is that you should be remembering or creating the answers in your mind, rather than just reading them out of your notes.

Recall Your Day at Night before Going to Sleep

It's easy to live your life and forget most of the individual days that make up a month, most of the months that make up the years, and so on, meaning we may remember very little in the end. Part of the reason this can happen is that many of our days may be quite similar. We tend to have routines – we get up at the same time, eat similar foods at the same meal times, go to work and leave work at the same times, and do the same general activities on a regular basis. This high level of routine can cause the days to blur together, making it difficult to distinguish them or remember them. But it's kind of sad, isn't it? To lack memory about your own life, and for a day to have no special significance….

Instead of allowing this memory fog to take over, it can help to do a daily review at night, and think back to the things that happened on any given day. What did you eat? What did you wear? Where did you go? Who did you see? What did you get done at work? These are some questions you might ask yourself, in reviewing your day.

As you might imagine, running through your day, playing it back in this way can have benefits beyond just training your memory. It can help you to see patterns in your life, and find things that are not going as well as you would like, so you can perhaps take action and make improvements.

An interesting thing about this exercise is that sometimes when I am running the day through my mind, I actually notice something new that I hadn't noticed earlier in the day. For example, you might notice when replaying through situations that you hurt someone's feelings. Perhaps you said something insensitive and they left the room afterward. At the time you didn't think anything about it. But recalling the memory, you realize it was something you said. Or you might recall that you promised to do a favor for someone, but that you completely forgot about it in the chaos of the day. This memory exercise can have the practical benefit of helping you to rebuild memories that you might have otherwise just completely forgotten. Then of course, you can take actions to fix any problems you identified.

What Happened the Last Time I Was Here?

Some people with very good memories can remember events very easily with cues in the environment. And having already visited a place can be a pretty strong cue, since most places don't change very much in appearance within a short time. As these people with great memories enter a familiar place, memories of their past interactions there come back without even intending to recall them.

Maybe some people remember such things automatically, but even if you don't, I believe asking "What happened the last time I was here?" can be a great memory training exercise. Most people tend to live in a single home, so it makes sense that you would visit some of the same places regularly. Perhaps you visit a relative, you go to a restaurant, a park, or anywhere. When you go to these familiar places, try to recall memories from a prior visit. If we use the restaurant example, what did you order last time? Who were you with? What waiter did you get? Where did you sit? What was the conversation about? What time of year was it when you last visited?

It should not be too difficult to at least remember something from the last visit, because there should be cues all around. It helps if you can remember where you sat. This alone may bring back memories of your waiter, what you ate, other people who sat next to you, and the general events of that visit.

What Did We Talk about Last Time?

When you meet a friend or acquaintance, whether planned or not, you can practice your memory by recalling what your last conversation was about. It can help to think about what you were doing together. Were you simply at work, at a gathering, or performing some kind of hobby, just talking on the phone, or what?

We may forget our conversations too easily because we don't always view them as especially important. When your friend talks to you about how his daughter doesn't want to brush her teeth at night, and all the things he's done to try to get her to do it, this may be easily forgotten if you don't have a daughter of your own you can relate it to, or if you are more concerned with your own problems. However, memories for events such as this are what help people bond and build deeper friendships. Now, this book isn't about bonding or friendships, it's about memory. However, one benefit of improving your memory is that you'll remember more about the people close to you, which will help strengthen those relationships. Imagine if you talk to that same friend a week later, and you ask if his daughter is finally brushing her teeth. When people actually pay attention and remember things about us, it makes us feel good. It's that simple. Another benefit of course is that remembering your last conversation will help to give you new material to talk about. Rather than searching for new and interesting topics, you can continue old conversations where you left off.

One way to help remember such conversations is to pay attention to the types of words used and to the inflection of the voice of the speaker. Ask yourself if they are proud, happy, sad, or disturbed? Don't just pay attention to *what* is said, but *how* it's said.

The more you practice remembering your last conversation, the longer you'll find you are able to remember. It's possible for a year or more to go by, and for you to actually recall what you were talking about at that time.

Hold that Thought

When someone else is talking, and a thought crosses your mind that is on a tangent, practice *not* interrupting the person right away. Instead, continue to listen to the person while holding your thought, of what you want to say as well. When they finish, you can go ahead and talk about how what they said reminds you of something else.

As a personal example, I often used to feel the need to say what came to mind right away, when a new thought crossed my mind in conversation. I would worry that if I didn't get it out, then I would forget my thought. Then, one of my friends with an excellent memory pointed out that if I try holding on to what I want to say, then I'll get better at it. She said it may take some practice, but the reason I may feel I'm not good at it is because I never do it, so I'm not well-practiced. In time, I learned to hold my thoughts while still paying attention to the conversation. This habit trains you to keep your memory active, improving the ability. Now, I routinely hold a thought while continuing to listen.

Sometimes, you'll talk to someone who has a lot that they want to say. Pay attention to what they say. Then, as they speak, you can also keep track of any of your own thoughts you want to bring up. As you begin this practice, keeping one thought in mind is good enough. In time, you may try to store two thoughts while listening to someone speak. Perhaps you can even build up to three. However, make sure you are able to pay attention to what is said. It doesn't make much sense to ask someone several questions of which they've already answered, which you missed because you were preoccupied with your own thoughts. The added benefit is if you practice this, you will interrupt people less in your general conversations.

Another reason to hold onto a thought, aside from conversations, is that the longer you keep something in mind, the more likely you are to actually remember it.

Unfortunately, many of us have the tendency to become distracted, or we move quickly from one task to the next, or one thought to the next. The problem is many of us are in a rush to learn, and a rush to remember, but this is a sort of contradiction. The more in a rush you are, the more likely you are to forget, because when you rush, you spend less time thinking about what you are doing.

How exactly you choose to hold your thoughts isn't especially important. It may involve simple reflection or repetition of what you want to remember. It could involve speculating as to how you could apply the information in some other context. You may just daydream or wonder about it, or ask questions about it in your own mind. You may even just associate this new memory with other things you already know.

Either way, holding onto that thought and memory will make it more vivid later on.

Mental Visual Search

This memory practice involves closing your eyes and doing a mental exploration of your room, or different places you are familiar with. Preferably, it is somewhere in your house or nearby where you can check your memory after you complete the exercise. The point of this exercise is simply to recall as much as you can about a given room or location.

In the fictional TV show *Psych*, the character Shawn pretends to have psychic abilities, but really he is just someone with extremely high observational and memory skills. In his childhood, his father often tested him to help build up his skills. One common test was that they would walk into a diner, sit down, and his father would ask him to close his eyes, and then quiz him on all kinds of details. For example, he might ask: What color hat is the person behind you wearing? What was the name of the waiter (that was on her name tag)? How many lightbulbs aren't lighting up properly? With frequent testing of this sort, his abilities were able to reach a point where he was observing and remembering things that most people would not pick up on.

Similarly as in *Psych*, this is an exercise you can use to practice your visual memory. I recommend practicing this without "studying" for it first. You should already be familiar with the area you are going to test yourself on, of course. Then you can simply make sure you are in a different room, and practice mentally visualizing everything from the test room.

Take your time to walk around in this mentally created

image of the room. Remember the type of furniture you have, the number of drawers, the clothes you have in the drawers, the pattern on your bed sheets, the books on your book shelf, with titles and author names, and so forth. Keep searching and searching, until you've remembered everything that you possibly can. Then, go back to the room and see how well you did.

Practice Remembering "N" Days Back (where N can mean one day, two days, three days, and so forth)

This training idea comes from a brain training software that has been used with the goal of improving working memory and intelligence. Working memory involves holding information temporarily in the mind, and processing it or applying it in some way. The software is called dual N-back. I'm not going to recommend the software itself, since it doesn't fit the theme of *Practical Memory*, but I am adapting the concept of the software into a practical exercise.

First, let's discuss a bit more about what dual N-back is.

Dual N-back is an application that presents you with two things at the same time, such as a number and letter, either visually or auditorily, but instead of needing to remember what you were just presented with, the software continues to steadily present you with new numbers and letters. Then it will ask you to remember what you were shown N steps back, and whether it was visually or auditorily presented. "N" can represent one, two, or three steps back, and so forth. This task is more difficult to do than you might imagine, since the software constantly shows you new numbers and letters, and does not give you a break to stop and catch up. Most people find this to be extremely difficult.

What I recommend is taking this concept and applying it to your daily life, which is much simpler and more practical. For example, you can practice thinking N days back, to strengthen your ability to remember back beyond just what has happened in the most recent moments. Remembering one day back in your life shouldn't be much of a challenge. However, it can be a useful starting point. You may practice remembering one day back at first. When you feel that your memories are pretty sharp for the prior day, you can practice remembering two days back. When you do well with that, you can go back further and further. Perhaps you could test yourself once a day, or a few times a week. When you have mastered one level, you can expand further back to give yourself a challenge. If you continue to train yourself, you may reach the point where you can clearly remember a week back, or even more.

When you practice recalling, you don't necessarily need to remember *everything* that happened in a given day. It may be more useful to choose something specific you will pay attention to. Perhaps you will keep track of what you eat, what clothes you wear, where you go, who you meet, which television programs you viewed, or something else. You can choose a specific task to remember, and then try to remember it N steps back. Again, start with one day back, then gradually build up to remembering further back. I believe a good goal is to remember back a full week.

Rearrange Your Items

Most of us naturally leave the same items in the same places most of the time. Especially those of us who are more organized. But even if not, you probably park your car in the same place, and put your utensils in the same place, right? For many items, when we move them somewhere new and unexpected, we are more likely to forget where we left them, especially if it is in an unusual place. Something that may surprise you is that most of the time, you are *not* remembering where you leave specific things at all. You are remembering where you leave that type of thing. For instance, office supplies are in the office room. DVDs are in the movie shelf by the TV. And plates are in the drawer of plates in the kitchen.

Obviously, being organized is a good quality, but an interesting way to practice your memory is to try moving your items into unexpected places, where you would not normally put them. However, moving things without reason isn't very practical. If you put your stapler in the freezer, it might test your memory, but you may break the stapler if you leave it in for too long, and also you probably don't need to go to that extreme to practice your memory. Instead, I would recommend moving things around a little bit. For example, if you normally keep your stapler in one office drawer, you can try moving it to another drawer. Later on of course, when you need that stapler again, you can stop and think where you left it, testing your memory.

To force yourself to exercise your memory, you can turn this into a habit if you like. With your everyday items that you use, such as a wallet, jacket, and keys, you can purposely choose to leave them in different areas of the house every day so that you actually need to think about where you left them, exercising your memory. Of course, keep in mind that memory isn't just something you use when you need to remember something. Really, you need to be mindful while you are putting these items down, paying attention to your actions, so you can remember them the next day. When you are changing things and putting items in new places, you need to be even more mindful.

Of course, the last thing we want to do is accidentally lose something while practicing our memory. To avoid losing any of these important items, I would recommend not hiding them, just moving them. Be sure that even if you forget where you put the item, that you could still find it fairly easily.

When ready to practice your memory, recall in your mind where you left the items, before you go searching for them. Searching for your items at random, even if you find them, is not an effective way to practice your memory.

Document Your Dreams in the Morning

Many people don't put much significance in their dreams. Sure, some stand out, but many of them slip away and seem to be forgotten forever. I usually only have a vague recollection of last night's dreams, with most of them slipping away in time. A few have been interesting enough that they stuck with me for months or years, but that is rare.

It may be a struggle to remember dreams, but that means it is a good thing to test. The more you struggle to recall, the more likely you are actually working out your memory muscles. Of course, memory is a part of your brain, not a muscle, but the analogy works similarly. To train your arm muscles, you would lift heavier and heavier weights, which of course are harder to lift. To train your memory, you should try to remember more. Keep in mind that those things which are harder to remember are good to help you advance in your abilities. Putting more effort, and straining at times, will help to make the connections stronger in your mind.

Dreams are often fuzzy and difficult to recall. Therefore, the best time to practice remembering them is first thing in the morning. This can simply be an exercise that you run through for a minute in the morning, to see what parts of the dreams you can recreate in your mind, or if you would like, you can take this further and write down what you recall. Writing it down will allow you to look back at your notes and relive the memory for years to come, at least with the aid of those notes.

Personally, I've noticed that if I get into a pattern of documenting dreams, that during that period my memories for dreams tend to improve. I've also noticed that when I meditate several times a week, that my memories for my dreams tend to improve as well. In fact, they seem to become much more vivid, which helps in remembering them. If you have trouble recalling your dreams, you may try to incorporate some of these tips.

BUILD NEW MEMORIES

A Brief Introduction

Building new memories is essentially what learning is all about. But this section isn't just about learning. It will give you tips on how to learn, understand, and remember. Often, we take in information and we assume that we are learning, but later on we have trouble remembering much of it. Part of the key to building new memories successfully is to have in mind exactly what it is that you want to remember. Without this intention, the memories will tend to evaporate, and we will lose our grasp on them.

A key point to understand here is that when we are learning, we shouldn't weigh everything equally, because the brain can only handle so much information. It is better to build an understanding of what is most important, and make sure to develop a solid understanding of those concepts.

Now, I will present you with more detailed tips on how to build new memories successfully.

Pay Attention and Be in the Present

We live in an age where it is more and more difficult to be in the present moment. We are often concerned with the past, the future, or some distraction that is pulling us in all directions. With too much chaos happening in the mind, and lack of focus or direction, it becomes more difficult to actually remember new experiences.

Practice being present

Paying attention and being in the present is a practice. The more you do it, the better you can get at this. If you have special challenges with keeping your mind in the moment, it could be useful to look into the practice of mindfulness or meditation. These will present you with techniques that can help bring you back to what is happening in the present moment. I've already stated that paying attention is important for memory, but how do you get yourself to pay attention? If you have problems with this, then it probably doesn't feel within your control. Your mind may just wander, whether you try to control it or not.

Practicing being present is the key. This is a practice, not an inherent trait that you are born with. The simple way to practice this would be to do any activity, such as going for a walk or having a conversation, and to make an effort to keep your mind on what is happening moment to moment. If your mind wanders to something else, or to the past or the future, you can guide yourself back to the present.

When you are able to successfully be in the moment, it means you will be processing what is happening in the most detail that you possibly can. You will be picking up on a lot of information, and you will be more likely to actually remember it later on. For example, if you notice someone smiling but sniffling and with watery eyes, you will remember that this person was probably sad but trying to hide it. Someone else who wasn't paying much attention, and not truly in the moment, will just see a normal happy person, even though this is incorrect.

By being totally present, you will gain a sharper view of the world, which will grant you a sharper memory.

Avoid multitasking and distraction

Much research has already established that when you multitask, you aren't fully processing the multiple things you are trying to do. Instead, your brain has to switch from one task to the other, and back again. And your brain is disrupted every time it switches, needing to catch up again to what it was doing earlier. This is inefficient.

Keep in mind that while multitasking you are likely to be absentminded, making more mistakes than you should because of a lack of attention. Also, you are essentially distracting yourself, limiting your full attention, which of course limits your memory. For things that are important that you want to remember later, don't multitask.

For any other distractions that you repeatedly experience, you should think about ways to reduce or eliminate them. Multitasking involves distractions that you choose. But there are also general distractions, which you do not choose. They are just there. However, both have negative effects on your attention and memory. Every time you are disrupted, and you return to what you were doing, you need to take some time to remember where you were.

For instance, Gloria Mark, a professor in the department of informatics at the University of California, Irvine, has studied how much time we lose when we get distracted. She says that when people are interrupted, it typically takes 23 minutes and 15 seconds to return to their work, and most people will do two intervening tasks before going back to their original project.

To make matters worse, you are much more likely to forget exactly what you were doing, which will waste time and force you to backtrack to an earlier point. It's quite likely you will need to re-do or rethink through things you had already finished, making you quite unproductive. Clearly, our best course of action is to focus on one task at a time, and keep distractions away when possible.

Plan to Remember (or have the intention to remember)

The importance of intending to remember was mentioned in the introduction, but this is such a key part of building new memories that I will elaborate upon that idea here.

When you plan to remember something, you make it much more likely that you will actually recall it. We can't pay attention to everything and remember it all, so a simple intention can come a long way in helping you to remember. Keep in mind that the brain tries to conserve its own energy. If something isn't even important enough for you to consciously intend to remember, the brain tends to file it under irrelevant stuff that you can easily forget. This means you will probably forget it.

Imagine if you were able to travel around with someone who had the perfect memory and never forgot anything. This would mean you could easily rely on this person any time you wanted to remember something. Rather than bother to remember something yourself, you could simply ask this person and they would recall it for you. This may sound nice, to not have to worry about remembering anymore. But by relying so much on this person, your memories would gradually get worse. You would count too much on this person, and you would never make any plans to remember anything, because you wouldn't need to. Therefore, you would forget much more than you should.

Rely on your own memory, and plan to remember. This will help you to remember much more.

Make it so you need to remember

You can plan to remember, but unless you truly *need* to remember, you may not be motivated enough to stick to your plan to remember something.

This reminds me of something a friend of mine told me. She has an extremely good memory, which she says she began developing at a very young age. As a child, her problem was that she often got into arguments with her mother, and her mother would always win those arguments because she conveniently had the "facts" to prove her case. My friend suspected something wasn't right, but her mom often said "You don't remember. I do. So I'm right." My friend had trouble defending herself, and she realized the problem was she couldn't remember everything she needed to. She started paying much closer attention after this, and was able to catch her mother saying things that couldn't be true, because she remembered that they happened differently. The point is that my friend felt the *need* to remember, and so she did. She couldn't stand to lose argument after argument, and so she did something about it. She paid attention to details, and practiced remembering them. To this day she has a superb memory for the words people say. Of course, this was the skill she developed which helped her to win arguments with her mother.

My friend felt the need to remember, but what if you don't? How can you create a need to remember?

One approach is to try to trick yourself into thinking that you must remember something, because someone is counting on you. Such false scenarios don't work well for me, but they might help you. The approach I tend to use is to actually plan to use the information in some way. For example, if watching a movie, think about what parts will be interesting to discuss when the movie ends, with your friends. If learning vocabulary words, plan to use them in your everyday conversation or in anything you may be writing. This creates a need for what you are learning or experiencing, rather than allowing it to become just some trivial event that you can easily forget.

Consider that you don't want to pressure yourself too much, or too little. With too much pressure you may forget things, because you will be too nervous. With too little pressure, you will also forget because the material won't seem important enough to remember. Create just the right level of need. Everyone has a different level that is right for them, so you must practice to figure it out.

Organize & Categorize

Organize and categorize your things in a way that makes sense to you. When you do this, it will be easier to remember where you left your items. For example, you are likely to find screwdrivers, wrenches, and pliers inside of a toolbox you may own, which you keep in the garage. Without having to strain your memory, you know where these things are. You don't have to ask if they could be in the kitchen or some other room. Most of us have some level of organization, because we understand how convenient this can be. It removes the burden from our memories of needing to remember where all sorts of random items are, scattered through the entire home. Clearly, it would make no sense to have a screwdriver in one room, pliers in another, and wrenches in another.

If you are wondering why I suggested moving items to unexpected places in a prior tip, yet here I suggest organizing, allow me to explain. The prior tip was to help you practice your memory and build it up by challenging it. This tip is intended to help you remember more information with less effort.

Making lists

Many of us do organize and categorize naturally, but when it comes to making lists, we often do not follow this principle. As an example, most people will have things they want to pick up at the grocery store, and so they will make one giant list of items they need to get. However, it probably makes more sense to group items together. For example, fruits and vegetables, toiletries, drinks, canned goods, etc. This is useful because grocery stores are grouped roughly into different categories, so this could make your trip easier. But also, if you wanted to memorize the list, or if by some chance you lost it, you would be much more likely to recall the items. Again, we tend to remember things better when they are grouped, rather than when they are all jumbled together without organization.

Another type of list many of us make are to-do lists. Usually when I read or hear about people making their to-do lists, they tend to put things in order of priority, but I actually prefer to make task groupings within my to do lists. For example, some general task groupings might be work, home life (e.g., chores), and fun & recreation. Then, these categories could be further divided into smaller ones if desired. Again, this is good for the sake of organization, but also for making it easier to remember these items yourself. As far as prioritizing goes, generally the groupings themselves have a certain level of priority. For example, the priority in the above example may be work, home life, then fun & recreation.

I believe this is a powerful tip. Don't underestimate the power of organization. If something is confusing to you, and therefore you are unable to build new memories effectively, start with finding an organizational system to start building a basic understanding. If everything is chaotic and completely disorganized for you, then you will not be able to form new memories, and your frustrations will just grow. Often, there isn't a natural organization, and you will need to figure it out for yourself.

This may involve organizing things by: priority, alphabetically, order, type, time or date, function, shape, size, physical composition, structure, impact, or some other way.

Choose an organizational scheme that makes the most sense to you. Find the patterns that are meaningful, and organize them in that fashion. For complicated things, I try to find a way to make sense of it using a spreadsheet such as excel, but it is difficult to give specific advice beyond this, as every topic is unique to learn and remember. If you think such a program may help you, there are plenty of tutorials available online on sites such as YouTube.

Don't confuse yourself

Avoid confusing yourself by establishing an organizational plan for where you place your items.

There is an amusing episode of *I Love Lucy* (an old program) where Lucy had a special item given to her, and she was so obsessive about hiding it in a good place that she ended up putting it in one place, moving it, putting it in another, moving it again, and so forth, over and over. She apparently wasn't satisfied with where she left it, so she kept moving it. By the next morning, she was in a frenzy because she couldn't remember where she had left this item that was so dear to her. She had confused her memory by moving the item so many times.

This is a sort of ridiculous situation, for the purpose of entertainment, but the lesson still holds. Have a plan for where you put your possessions, and why you put them there, to avoid always storing things in seemingly random places that you cannot remember.

Make it Personal

Whatever it is you wish to remember, your motivation to remember will influence your ability to do so. One way to help with this is to turn what you want to remember into something personally relevant to you. If it isn't naturally relevant, you need to find a way to make it so. This may take a bit of creativity, but when you find that personal relationship with what you want to remember, your memory will benefit greatly.

In general, this tip applies more when we are required to remember something because of school or work, but where studying and learning it feels like drudgery. This happens sometimes. For those things where you are already 100% motivated and interested, you won't need to worry about remembering. It will happen easily because you are interested and focused. As you can see, if you were able to actually make yourself motivated by making it personal, the remembering part would be much easier.

I once had a teacher who made a good point about memory. He said:

Many of you students tell me you can't remember what I teach. You can't remember the presidents, or important dates in history, and so forth. But I hear you singing your favorite songs in the halls. Apparently you've been able to memorize those. Don't tell me you can't remember what I teach. This may not be fun or entertaining to remember, but you are fully capable of it.

I believe a key way to make things more fun and relevant so we can remember them, is to simply make it personal. Students remembered the songs because it meant something to them personally, whereas they struggled to find the relevance in their class material.

Imagine yourself in their place

A straightforward example where people naturally tend to put themselves in another's place, is when reading a novel. You will probably put yourself in the position of the hero or the main character, and you will think through how you would react to the circumstances if you were in the same position.

Reading a novel is an area where you may naturally look for the personal relevance, or put yourself in the shoes of the hero, but you can do this with other areas of your life too. If someone is telling a story, you can put yourself in their position and imagine how you would handle it. If you are watching a movie, you can do the same, and for other situations as well.

Something to be cautious of is that instead of paying attention and making it personally relevant, you may be reminded of your personal experiences. Unfortunately, reliving your personal experiences is not necessarily a helpful way to build new memories. For example, if I tell you a story about the first time I caught a fish, you may relate it back to the first time you did the same thing too. This is fine, but the problem is if you were to get caught up in thinking or talking too much about your own experience, instead of listening to the story

I wanted to tell you. When building memories, you need to keep your focus outward. You may relate personal aspects of your experience, but remember that ultimately you are trying to retain information from the world around you.

Search for the personal relevance

Sometimes, we think that something does not relate to us, and so we stop caring. It is important to search further. Don't just accept that something has no relation to you. This reminds me of the high school student that might be disinterested because nothing they are learning seems to matter for their personal lives. In such a case, it can be difficult to find out why the material matters, but it is important to seek out those personal connections.

For example, if chemistry seems irrelevant, perhaps learn about the chemical properties of things that you do care about to make it more relevant. Maybe chemistry seems dead to you, being about lifeless molecules. Then you may wish to jump into organic chemistry (which pertains to living organisms) to spark your interest.

The key point here is that if you read or hear about something that seems to have no significance to you, seek out a way to make it personally relevant. This isn't always easy, but it is much better to spend some time up front and discover that personal relevance, instead of hating the process of remembering something. This can take some effort and work, but it will be a critical step in helping you to remember new things.

Process through All of the Senses

We all know what the senses are, but as a refresher, they are to see, touch, taste, smell, and hear. These senses are our main ways of experiencing the world, and so obviously they are pretty important in forming new memories. We should make it a point to remember to use all of them in our daily lives, because each one is a unique window to be able to build new memories from.

Use multiple senses to deepen your memory

When you experience something new, it will aid your memory to focus on taking it in through many of your senses, not just one. If you limit yourself to always experiencing new things with just sight, for example, then you are reducing the number of stimuli that could cue a memory. Consider if you were to experience something with all five of your senses. It would then become practically impossible to forget. At minimum, I would suggest shooting for experiencing new things with at least two of your senses. Even if you are reading a book, you can use multiple senses because you can imagine and recreate them.

The above paragraph deals with when you are first experiencing something new. What about later, when you wish to actually recall your memories? That is when you will be thankful if you processed through multiple senses. If you did, you should recall the memory much more easily. But consider a case where you struggle to remember, perhaps because you formed the memory years ago. To help recall it, you will simply need to ask yourself about the various senses. How did it taste? How did it feel? What did it look like? How did it smell? Did it make any noise or sound? All of these senses will provide a pathway to help you remember something more clearly.

Depth & Redundancy

If you struggle to remember something time and time again, it can help to dig deeper and learn more thoroughly. Rather than getting stuck on the surface levels of what you want to remember, sometimes we need to search deeper to gain an understanding and build stronger memories.

Another option is to learn the same thing in a different way. Perhaps instead of only learning through books, you can experience something firsthand. Or instead of just learning from one teacher, you can also get a tutor who explains the material differently. Adding redundancies such as this to your learning will help better establish your memories.

Depth

When struggling to remember something, consider going deeper into the topic. When you are stuck on a surface level, sometimes things just don't make that much sense. Or the topic may feel dry and uninteresting at a basic level, but when you dig deeper you discover that it is actually fascinating.

As an example, perhaps you want to understand the periodic table of elements, but it all seems lifeless for you and you struggle to learn anything. This could be because the amount of protons, neutrons, and the element names seem meaningless to you. In such a case, it could make sense for you to dig deeper. You might decide to learn about the history of the periodic table. You could also learn how the first elements were discovered, or other background key facts. Perhaps you will even discover why it is organized the way that it is, and learn patterns that help you to remember the table. By learning more deeply, this will help you find meaning in what you are learning, and make it more likely for you to remember much more.

It is easy to forget a few surface level facts, but when we learn deeply, we will build an understanding and ultimately remember much more.

Redundancy

Sometimes when a topic is overly difficult to remember, it may mean that trying to make the same connection in your mind over and over simply isn't working. Perhaps you have tried so many times that now when you review the material, you don't really expect to remember, and also, you do so in a mindless fashion because you are truly bored. In this case, making the material new can help. You can do this by adding redundancies. This just means to learn the same thing, but in a different way. This can be as simple as if you are using flash cards, to test yourself in the opposite way. For example, if recalling the definition based on the word, practice recalling the word based on the definition instead.

Another form of redundancy would be to learn the same material through different senses, approaches, formats, or even different books that cover the same topic. The point is to get more exposure in ways that present basically the same thing, but in different forms. It's possible that you may not understand something too well when you try to learn it one way, but it may just click and make sense when presented in a different way. Also, the mere repetition of the material can help you to remember it better.

As a real life example of this, I once tutored a student, who even though she was around 15 years old, had never learned her multiplication tables. She told me she had given up on it. I was surprised because she seemed like a fully capable student. She confessed that numbers didn't make any sense to her, and no matter how many times she wrote them out, she wasn't able to recall them. But she mentioned that she could deal with words much better. I ended up recommending that she write out the tables in the form of words instead of numbers. Instead of 3 x 5 = 15, it would be three times five equals fifteen. After this change, she began to make progress on learning them quite fast. Words made sense to her, whereas numbers did not.

Sometimes, one way of processing information doesn't fit our memory abilities or our understanding, and we need to look at the information in a deeper way, or in a different way (redundancies).

Use Big Interest Points as Anchors to "Hang" New Memories on (as if on a coat hanger)

What are you really interested in that you've loved for a long time? Is it music, dinosaurs, shopping, art, video games? This could involve your profession, but it doesn't have to. It may just be something you have fun doing, or something you've been almost obsessive about, perhaps. It could also include memory talents. For example, are you especially good at remembering numbers, dates, faces, locations, scents, or anything like this?

With this tip, you will frame new memories in the context of your strengths.

I met a professor once who made a pretty good analogy, that forming new memories is like coat hangers. This may sound strange, but he meant that a coat hanger can represent a solid memory that you have. And your goal is to "hang" any new memories you are trying to form, to these solid memories. His point was that new memories need to be hung, or related in some way to old memories that you already have. Practically speaking, you should find those very strong memories, those things you love, are passionate about, talented in, and so forth, and hang your new memories onto that. This will allow you to form new memories more quickly, and you will not forget them as easily.

How does this new thing relate to your interest points, or your strengths?

When you are learning something new that you want to remember, ask yourself how it relates back to your strengths. This is an especially useful strategy when what you want to remember is dry or if it is boring you. For me, some of my strengths are in psychology, chess, and music, so I might try to tie in a new topic I learn to one of these. For example, if I'm learning history, I could ask what type of music was playing in the time period or region. I have a generally wide interest in music, so this would be a way to make it fun.

There are some books which conveniently relate different topics with each other, and can help you to remember the material better. For instance, I once read a book called *The History of the World in 6 Glasses*, which related beverages to history. This seems like it would be the perfect book for someone who could appreciate various drinks (e.g., coffee, tea, beer, wine), but who found it difficult to get engaged with learning history.

Sometimes, it can be a bit of a struggle to find a way to relate your interests to whatever you are trying to learn, but it is well worth the effort as it makes the process to remember new information much easier.

I recommend mixing up your interests and how you relate them to new things, so you are not always searching for relationships to just one topic. First of all, it can become boring to always relate new topics to just one familiar one. Second, you are limiting the types of connections you can make if you are only comfortable with one topic. Also, keep in mind that some topics relate to each other more easily than others (e.g., perhaps dance and music relate more easily than botany and physical therapy). You'll generally be more successful with building memories when you have many areas that interest you. If you don't feel especially strong in many topics, I would recommend very gradually building up your understanding in a few different areas. Focus on one expertise at a time, however, as you will make progress more quickly this way.

Limit Your Information Intake

This may seem like a strange tip, to limit your information. Many of us want to remember more. That is why we read books such as this. But a key thing to understand is that you cannot remember everything. Throwing more information at you will just overwhelm your memory, making it more likely that you will come away knowing and understanding nothing. You will want to avoid such an information overload.

Be more intensive, and less extensive with what you want to remember

To be extensive with your information intake means that you seek out a wide range of information from many, many outlets. It can be good at times to seek out information broadly, but a problem is that if you are jumping from topic to topic too often, then you aren't allowing yourself the chance to truly understand it. The information you pick up may just appear to be superficial and turn into disconnected facts in your mind, making it more difficult to hold on to and actually remember.

The intensive way of taking in information is to delve deeper into a topic. This will likely involve spending more time with one particular source. It may be a news article, someone you are interviewing, a book, or any sort of information. The key point is that you find a piece of information that is highly important and that is worth going through multiple times. This will allow you to look at it more deeply, learn it, and take the time to memorize certain parts and reflect on their meaning, to apply the principles for yourself, and so forth.

An example of this may be reading a quote, and thinking through how the quote applies in your life, any alternative meanings it may have, why the message has been considered so important as to be quoted time and again, etc. Or another example would be to read a book, think about it deeply, take notes on it, put it aside, then come back to it after several months later and re-evaluate your opinions of it.

How do these two styles fit together? Perhaps you can be extensive at first, when you are searching for something that is truly worth your time. You can search broadly, looking for a wide variety of information that interests you. Then, when you find one source that seems especially helpful, you can study it more deeply. At that point, you would spend much more time on it, and give it your full attention. Since you know this material is important, spending more time with it will most likely pay off in your greater understanding and recollection of it.

Focus on the 80/20 rule of what you want to remember

The 80/20 rule, or the Pareto principle, just means that roughly 80% of your effects tend to come from 20% of the causes.

Therefore, you should focus more time and energy on that critical 20% of actions you can take which will have the biggest effects.

Imagine that you have a tsunami of things that you are trying to learn and focus on. It may be a massive amount of reading material, a new skill, or some kind of data. The best way to proceed then is to identify the most important parts that you can learn, and to focus on those. There is a limit to how much you can take in and reasonably remember, so you want to be efficient. This means if you have the option of going with a variety of information sources, you should search for the few that will give you the most benefit, with the least fluff.

For example, if you can read a book that is a thousand pages, but has the same information as a book of 500 pages, you should probably go with the shorter one. Or if you can read an article instead of a lengthy book that covers the same thing, it may be best to simply read the article. This will help you to learn more in less time.

If you struggle to find that 20% of information that is most important, and that will tell you 80% of what you really need to know, consider the quote by Gary Keller in his book *The One Thing*. He says:

> **"What's the ONE Thing you can do such that by doing it everything else will be easier or unnecessary?"**

I like this quote not only because it makes a good point, but because it can also be applied to memory. Here is a form of the question, applying it to memory:

> **"What is the ONE thing you can remember that will make remembering everything else easier or unnecessary?"**

For example, some people I have met who are fantastic at math have been highly skilled at applying this principle. Rather than sit around memorizing *everything* in a textbook, they tend to memorize the *key rules* they need to know, from which they can figure out everything else they will need to know. This not only saves them time, it also builds their understanding which effectively gives them a better memory. Instead of truly needing to remember every detail in a textbook, they understand it well enough to figure things out as needed – which in the end is just about as useful as remembering it.

Slow Things Down

Some people talk very fast, and if you are trying to remember what they say, this can be a big barrier to successfully recalling it. To remember something that is said, often you need to have a moment to process it, visualize it, or consider the context as it is being said. If it goes too fast and you can barely pick up what a person is saying, you will obviously fall behind, miss things, and fail to remember later on.

Remember the importance of attention, and of actually experiencing something new to its fullest. If you have not been able to capture a memory in the first place, then you will never be able to remember it later. It will just be fuzzy, as you cannot recall what you never really picked up on in the first place. Much of the time, we are not actually forgetting anything. We simply never learned or captured the experience to begin with.

In today's age, this principle seems especially important. Most of us are in a rush. We want to get to the end point faster and faster. We want to achieve our goals, and view the process to get there as an obstacle. The reality is we can become our own enemy if we are in too much of a rush. Sometimes the best way to speed up is to slow down, take the time to learn, remember, and understand. Then, in time you will become faster, more efficient, and build expertise.

Put it in slow motion

Imagine a novice fighter watching Bruce Lee videos – one of the most expert and fastest martial artists who ever lived. Even if you watched a massive amount of his fighting videos, you would still not understand or remember his moves. He's too fast. To really learn and understand what he is doing, it would probably be best to watch his videos in slow motion. This would allow you to pick up on finer details that you would otherwise miss. When you have trouble learning and remembering something new, put it in slow motion instead of trying to go too fast.

You may not be working with video, but that is okay. To put something in slow motion, just run through the process slower. When reading, review the material slower, and look through graphics and images in detail. Or when practicing a skill, do it slower if you can, focusing on nailing down the technique precisely, rather than on going faster.

Repeat it to yourself

If you feel that someone is talking too fast, you can slow things down by repeating it yourself, and checking if you were right. People sometimes talk very fast, and if this gives you trouble for keeping up and remembering, you can slow down the pace by stopping them for a moment and repeating what they say. This can work whether the information involves a list or just general information. If they get annoyed, simply mention that you are trying to make sure you understood correctly. What teachers, or people who already understand a topic sometimes forget is that when you are learning something new, sometimes it is like learning a foreign language. You need a bit of extra time to pick everything up. Whereas because of their expertise, they are capable of talking through big ideas quite fast. Don't be afraid to slow them down through repeating what they have said.

Clarify it yourself with comments and questions

Rather than repeating what they just said, you could simply attempt to clarify your understanding of the information. This is when you say something like "Oh, so you mean…" and you attempt a sort of paraphrase or clarification of uncertain parts, to make sure that you actually did get everything. You may also simply ask a straightforward question. These sorts of tactics slow things down so you can pick up details and have extra time to remember and understand more fully.

You do not want to make the mistake of standing by idly while someone is explaining complex or difficult ideas. Do not let them keep on talking if you are getting lost. It is important that you make comments or ask questions to help make sure that you are keeping up. Sometimes, we misunderstand something without even knowing. By making occasional comments and asking questions, you can help make sure that you are indeed keeping up and understanding.

Ask them to repeat it, and to slow down

Obviously, you can also ask the person you are listening to, to simply slow down. You may let them know that this is important to you and you want to make sure you get everything they say. This should get them to go at least a bit slower. But realize most people speak the way they do out of habit, so if they begin to speed up again, it is okay to ask them to slow down once again.

Break Things down into Chunks

As we have already discussed, the human memory is not unlimited. We can only make sense of so much new information at a time. Keep your goals realistic. Rather than trying to remember huge amounts of information, it can help to break it down into smaller pieces.

Consider a research study conducted by Adriaan de Groot on chess experts and chess amateurs. Both groups were asked to memorize a variety of chess positions found in *typical games*, and only given a few seconds to do it. The chess experts did very well on remembering these positions because they had familiarity with them. Those unfamiliar with chess performed poorly.

In a follow up study conducted by William Chase and Herbert Simon, the experts and non-experts were both given *random* chess positions to memorize. In this case, the experts only performed slightly better than the non-experts in remembering positions. This is believed to have happened because even in random positions, occasionally some familiar pattern might have accidentally emerged, giving the experts an advantage.

A big conclusion from observing how the experts remembered more came from realizing that the experts saw things in terms of chunks. Because they understood the game at a deeper level, they could remember several pieces grouped together in some form as a single chunk. To explain this in another form, the sentence "The boy and the girl played together in the yard" is probably very easy to remember, and might be viewed as a single chunk of information. However, if you think of it, that is 10 words. Many people would struggle to remember 10 random words. Also, it's 39 letters, which I'm certain most people would not be able to remember 39 random letters.

Yet when the information makes some sense to us, we are able to recognize it as a single chunk.

For this reason, never downplay understanding as being less important than pure memory. They are both important. The greater your understanding, the better you will be able to remember more information in less time, as the chess experts were able to do in the above studies.

Learn one chunk, then the next, then the next...

I used to take piano lessons, and my instructor stressed the importance of learning one measure (which is a chunk of notes), then moving onto the next measure, learning that one, and onward. He emphasized not to move forward until I had fully learned one measure. I took his advice, and through this process, I would memorize how to play entire songs fairly quickly. However, I noticed that when I tried to advance too quickly through the measures, that I wasn't able to remember very much at all. It was important to follow what he said precisely, and go step by step, measure by measure.

Similarly, in your daily life, focus on one sequence of information at a time. If you try to take it all in at once, then it will turn into a chaotic blur, making it seem meaningless, and soon the information will be lost to you. The analogy of food comes to mind. You wouldn't try to swallow your whole meal at once. Instead, you go bite by bite. Similarly, you shouldn't force yourself to take in too much information. It just doesn't make sense because you probably won't remember any of it later.

Routines Result in Forgetfulness

Routines can be good because we can create patterns in our lives of the most important things that we need to do. But it turns out that for our memories, too much routine can be bad. The more routines we have, the less anything stands out in our minds, and the less we tend to exercise our memories, which can weaken our abilities.

Try new things

I believe there is a lot of power in routines, so I wouldn't advise you to eliminate all routine from your life. Instead, what I would advise you to do is to try new things. We have all heard this advice. But not only can it help you to move beyond your comfort zone, it can also be a good way to stimulate your memory. When we do the same things day in and day out, our memories start to blur together. However, when we enter new settings, our memories become hyperactive. If you expose yourself to a high level of new stimulation, the brain seems to sense that it will probably need to remember more. At minimum, it will need to work harder to try to remember new things. However, in familiar and repetitive environments, the mind can fall into a sluggish state. It feels that it knows what it needs to, and that remembering anything more is unnecessary.

If you wonder why doing something new may stimulate memories, the answer is apparently chemical in nature. For instance, Dr. Mark Williams in an article "Specific Ways to Improve Your Memory" in *Psychology Today* has stated:

> *By creating new experiences we stimulate our brain and a substance called brain-derived neurotrophic factor or BDNF. Other things that stimulate BDNF include exercise and eating curcumin, part of the Indian spice turmeric that is used in curry. BDNF is vital to memory and helps nerve cells grow and connect. BDNF levels are low in Alzheimer's disease and Huntington's disease where the genetic defect seems to result in low BDNF levels. Stimulating BDNF is part of the biochemical underpinning of our memory maintenance and improvement strategies.*

How can we actually stimulate BDNF to improve our memories? According to Dr. Williams it's simple. Try new things, or you can also exercise and eat food with turmeric.

More involved ways to try new things would be to travel somewhere new, or engage in a new type of experience you never tried, perhaps going to the theater, a musical, museum, concert, or taking a dance or martial arts class. Anything that is a completely new form of experience you hadn't taken part in before, would fit here.

However, you don't need to take such large steps if you lack the time or interest. Less dramatic ways to do something new may involve simply doing something outside of your normal routine. Perhaps you would go to a new restaurant, see a new movie, read a different kind of book, talk with an old friend you hadn't seen in a while, cook a new recipe, and so forth. If it falls out of your normal routine, then it is new.

Use Wild or Shocking Imagery with Action

Imagining events in a wild or shocking way makes it much more likely that you will actually remember them. Then, if you add action to these images, turning them into a short video clip inside your mind, you will make them even more memorable. We struggle to remember events that are too routine, but those that shock us in some way, we tend to remember.

Practice making the ordinary into the extraordinary

If I meet someone, and she tells me her name is Miranda and she likes to run, maybe I want to remember that she runs so I can mention something about it the next time I talk to her. In order to remember this, I might envision her dressed like the DC Comics superhero, the Flash, in an orange suit with a lightning bolt in front. By the way, his super speed apparently allows him to run faster than a speeding bullet. With this knowledge, I could also imagine her running so fast that she turns into a bullet. These visuals are more dramatic and extraordinary, so I am much more likely to remember this than if I just picture her in running gear jogging around the neighborhood.

Of course, not everyone is used to visualizing in this way, so it can take a bit of practice. When someone says something that you want to remember, or you read something you want to remember, just take a moment to turn it into wild image, and add action to it. You don't need to spend too much time creating the images. The main feature is that they should be shocking and convey something that you want to remember.

Declutter your Environment

Having less clutter tends to mean that you will have less to remember, which can help you to remember the things that do matter. Often, we have trouble recalling not because our memories are bad, but because our environments and therefore our minds are so overstuffed with objects, people, and ideas. It helps to declutter and clear the mind, to make space to remember more.

Avoid too much junk information

Do you realize how much information is pumped into our heads every single day? I wouldn't know. I no longer even notice whether ad block is installed on my computer or not, because I have a mental filter where I automatically do not pay attention to ads. But that is just on the computer. And that is only for those old-fashioned type of ads that are just a picture with a link, such as a banner. Even so, ad makers get more and more crafty year by year. On Facebook, I can't even tell the difference between a normal post and an ad, much of the time, other than that the ads say "sponsored". To me, it's all just content – some useful, some not.

Unfortunately, much of what we are exposed to (both online and offline) is junk information, meaning commercials, advertisements, pop-ups, junk mail, rumors and gossip, and other irrelevant stuff. These are things which are not especially important or relevant to our lives, but they take up our attention and memory. Whether we realize it or not, junk information tends to suck away our mental energies, draining our abilities. For this reason, we should do what we can to reduce it or eliminate it from our lives, and make more room for what truly matters.

Avoid too much junk in your environment

Some people can handle a great deal of complexity and manage it all in their lives. But if you find that there is too much junk around you and you struggle to remember where you left things, because they could be just about anywhere, then it is probably time to start getting rid of some of the excess things that you own.

Decluttering your physical space often has an impact on decluttering your mind. A messy space can make for a chaotic mind, and a clear space can make for clear thinking. The point here is not to be too harsh on those who are a bit on the messy side, as some research has actually supported that a messier space can aid creativity. But keep in mind that being too messy could have a negative impact on your memory. When things are simpler and better organized, we remember them better than when they are disordered.

Remember Your Notes

When taking notes, for a class, a lecture, or in a meeting, when you are finished you may find that you have pages of notes, but that you didn't have the time to organize them during your note-taking. Everything may be all jumbled together, and perhaps you are not even sure of what is important anymore. Afterward, your memory could be a bit hazy, since you were so busy taking notes, and not able to pay close attention at the same time.

When we take notes, especially if there are a lot of notes such as for a course or on a meeting, it's easy to get overwhelmed with the material. In the moment of taking notes, it can be difficult to determine what is important to remember above all else. However, it may not be quite as difficult as you would think. Here are some tips to help you remember your notes.

Put a checkbox next to actionable items

I used to have this problem often – where I felt that my notes were horrible and unhelpful, and that I didn't have a great organization or memory for the things that I needed to know. As you can imagine, this was frustrating because I felt like I had wasted my time taking bad notes. To top it off, my handwriting isn't very good, because I tend to write very fast, in efforts to make sure that I don't miss anything important.

When I mentioned this to a highly logical computer engineer, he told me that the problem was quite simple. He said the notes that are usually the most important are the ones that you need to take action on. Put a checkbox next to those, so you can tell at a glance what you actually need to do. These might be things the boss asked you to take care of, or it could be an assignment that is due soon, or some other errand you need to do.

It's much easier to remember what you need to do when your notes clearly show you. You won't need to struggle through reading pages of notes to figure it out later. I saw an immediate boost the quality of my notes, my memory, and my understanding, from implementing this advice.

Use asterisks for other important items

What about other important items that aren't necessarily actions you need to take? If you notice something very important that you want to be sure to remember, I recommend a two asterisk system. For important notes, put an asterisk next to the line. For essential notes that you absolutely need to know, you can put two asterisks. This of course doesn't automatically mean you will remember it. But it will be a big help, because when you review your notes later, you can pay special attention to those important notes.

The point of these systems, of putting checkboxes and asterisks next to your notes as you go, is that it's quite likely that many of your notes are not especially important. Rather than allow your mind to wander, you need to focus so that you when you look at your notes later, you immediately know the most important things that you need to do or understand.

When You Get Lost While Someone Else Is Talking, Return to Where You Were

Sometimes the mind can wander while someone else is talking to us. If it only happens for a few seconds, it's usually easy to continue listening. But if you wander off and begin to daydream while someone else is talking, you can get quite lost, not picking up what the person has just said. When this happens, you won't be able to remember much of anything that was said. Here are some tips to help avoid such problems.

Backtrack to where you were

When you do get lost in a conversation, allowing the person to continue talking on the belief that you can figure everything out as you go, can be a mistake. To allow the person to continue will just make it so you get more and more lost, most likely.

In fact, you should tell the person right away that you didn't understand something, or you can simply ask them to repeat a fact or to clarify what you missed. If you admit that your attention slipped, or that you missed everything said in the past minute, they may be annoyed, but they will be more annoyed when you sit there for 10 minutes without understanding or remembering much of anything.

The analogy is similar to if you get lost somewhere. It is worse to keep going deeper and deeper, denying that you have gotten lost, as the problem will just get worse. Instead, you have to acknowledge what has happened and try to fix it by understanding where exactly the confusion happened.

Explain it and Teach it

Explaining and teaching some material is a good way to reestablish it in your memory. Essentially, this is a way of reviewing your memories by going through it with someone else. Beyond just aiding memory, I've personally had the experience of reaching a higher level of understanding while explaining something to someone else. This is often when I come to new realizations that I probably would not have otherwise had.

Find someone you can teach or tutor

If you have someone who is willing to listen, who knows less about a topic than you, you could try to explain it to them. You could actually try this practice on your own, explaining things out loud to yourself, or in your own mind, but it is more valuable to do it with someone else. This is because they will often ask questions, which you should encourage. Those questions will test what you know, and force you to exercise your memory. Anything you are not sure how to answer will point to an area that you need to spend more time on learning and understanding.

RECOVER "LOST" MEMORIES

A Brief Introduction

One of the more interesting aspects of memory is when you know that there is something stored in your brain that you want to recall, but it feels like it is lost. The troubling thing is you can remember that at one point you knew this piece of information. You know you should be able to remember, which makes it more frustrating. Unfortunately when this happens, most of us just become frustrated, unsure of how to recall the memories.

Sometimes, these memories will come back on their own. If the memory is in your brain somewhere, and you made an effort to look for it, then your subconscious may continue to search for this lost memory. However, this section isn't about getting your memories back by chance or subconsciously. There are actually systems or strategies you can apply if you want to improve your chances of recovering a lost memory.

If you do have some lost memories you want to get back, keep in mind that this is no easy task. The best results may come from combining some of the following strategies, rather than relying on just one.

Struggle to Remember

As unexpected as this tip may be, the more you struggle to find a memory, the more likely you are to find it. Then, if you are able to get it back, you will be more likely to continue to remember it later on. Even if you don't remember what you wanted to, this struggle helps establish how important the memory is, and makes it more likely that you will recall it later.

Don't give up too easily

Don't spend just five seconds trying to remember something and then give up. If the memory is important to you, take longer and try to find it. I've noticed a habit in many people who claim they are not good at something. Whether it is memory or anything else, they often get into a cycle of giving up too early on what they want to accomplish. This is because they expect to do poorly, and so they give up *without* putting in much effort, sabotaging themselves, which then results in failure. Actually struggling through, and trying to remember for a longer time, is a way to prove to yourself that you can actually remember. Ultimately, if you do this you will improve in your ability to remember.

Some of the people I know with better memories are willing to truly struggle through the process of remembering. They will tend to search deeper and deeper, unwilling to give up on what they want to remember. Often, I feel like it actually pains them *not* to remember. They may become slightly obsessive about the need to recall the memories that they struggle to find, meaning they spend much more time trying to recover them. I have heard these people say, if they are unable to recall a memory, something like "that's going to bother me the rest of the day". What I take this to mean is that they may periodically think back to this memory throughout the day, being unwilling to let it go. This makes them much more likely to remember than the rest of us who may give up too fast.

Remembering even when you think you have forgotten

When I was an undergraduate student at Purdue University, sometimes I received a written essay exam and I wasn't confident that I knew some of the answers. However, I was highly dedicated to doing the best that I possibly could. First, I would answer all of the questions that I was sure I knew. For the rest that I wasn't sure if I knew them, I would skip them for the moment, and come back to them after I answered the questions I was certain about.

Generally, I studied and prepared pretty well for exams, so I usually felt that all of the correct information had to be somewhere in my head. I recall being surprised several times, to find that the more I struggled to find an answer, the more I did tend to actually arrive at a correct solution. There were many exams where I initially felt quite uncertain that I knew the answers, but with my system of struggling through, I would ultimately remember most of the material that I needed. I am sure that we can remember much more than we actually think we are capable of, as I proved this to myself many times while taking exams.

Search Your Memories by Theme

I used to work with a professor who would occasionally pause if a question was asked, and he would say "Hold on, I'm doing a search." He would then look at the wall perhaps five or ten seconds, and having recalled the memories he needed, proceed to give some advice or answer a question. He was a very bright professor, and I would imagine his mind working as some kind of search engine, finding all of the relevant memories he needed.

He seemingly had an ability to retrieve any memory at will, just by doing his "search".

What if we could all do something like that? Well, maybe we can. I believe the trick is to search in themes. This helps prevent us from getting stuck on being unable to find that memory we want.

Instead of remembering the actual thing you want to remember, recall themes

Recalling the specific thing that you want to remember is often quite difficult. You can't seem to find it, no matter what you try. So how do we recover those more difficult memories that seem to have escaped us? We shift our focus away from trying to remember this one thing, and instead look at themes that relate to what we want to remember. It seems counterintuitive, but this can be highly effective.

As an example, I recently saw a variety of films in a fairly short period. I saw *La La Land*, *Nocturnal Animals*, and another film I could not recall. These were all films I had seen with one friend, and after some time passed, we only remembered two of them. We couldn't remember the last one, so it occurred to me that instead of trying to remember the movie itself, without any real clues, that maybe I could think of genres of movies. Maybe if I could remember the right genre, this would help me to remember the movie we saw.

So I went through some in my mind… romantic, comedy, horror…. When I got to horror, the category felt right, and I quickly realized that the movie we had seen was *Split*, a horror type of film.

Try this the next time you are stuck trying to remember something that fits into a category like a book or a movie.

Simply recall different categories it might fit into. When you hit the right category, your mind will light up and you should easily be able to recall the memory you wanted.

Keep in mind that if you are desperate to remember something and even themes are difficult to recall, you can always Google them or search Wikipedia for a list of relevant themes / topics / genres.

Listen to Music That Relates to What You Want to Remember

Music that was played at significant moments, or which somehow comes to represent significant periods, tends to bring us back to that time when we heard the music. It gives us a powerful ability to recall effortlessly. The music itself is such a powerful cue that it brings other related memories rushing in, whether you wanted them to emerge or not.

Spark memories with music

Growing up, I remember my father sometimes saying that listening to songs from the 60s would bring him back to where he was in life at that point. It would bring the memories flooding back. I got the sense that it brought back not just images, but a full picture of what his life was like, what the general feeling was, and so forth.

As a child I didn't understand too well, but now I understand what he meant better. I enjoy music a lot, and I listen to a wide variety on the free streaming site, Spotify. Sometimes, I will look for musical groups that I used to listen to at different phases of my life. And of course, listening to that music does bring me back to where I was at that point. I'll remember what I was doing, what I was thinking, what I was feeling, and many details about my life at that time.

I recommend finding some music from prior times in your life and listening to it, to help bring back memories that would otherwise seem lost.

Recent discoveries are showing us that music is actually more powerful than we had previously thought. For example, I recently saw a fascinating video of an older man with Alzheimer's disease who was given music, to help stimulate his memories. If you are interested, the documentary that includes this story and many others is called *Alive Inside*, and is available via Aliveinside.org or YouTube.

In the video, there is an older man named Henry who could not seem to answer even basic "yes" or "no" questions. He appeared to be generally inactive and unresponsive. Then, someone played music from when he would have been a younger man, and his eyes lit up. Before he had seemed dormant, and now he was wide awake, completely engaged and active. He began to sing and dance along with the music. After the song finished, he was asked questions about music and his life. Surprisingly, he was actually able to communicate quite well, as if a normal person without memory issues. It was as if he had been lying dormant within this body, and the music had such a powerful effect that he remembered who he was, and he felt alive again.

This isn't necessarily a rare event, as many lives have now been impacted through music. As can be seen in *Alive Inside*, music has helped *many* people with dementia to "come alive" and to remember their past.

Why would music help us to remember, even for persons with dementia? The late Dr. Oliver Sacks has said that "music has more ability to activate more parts of the brain than any other stimulus." It seems that this ability to activate so many parts of the brain all at once aids people in remembering without much effort.

If music is powerful enough to help even dementia patients, I believe it could be a helpful memory tool for the rest of us as well.

Seek out Scents That Relate to What You Want to Remember

Similarly as with music, scents have been known to have a powerful effect on our memories. With either music or scents, they can create a sort of "involuntary memory" effect, where the memories come flooding back, whether we want them to or not. This is interesting because often we have to struggle to remember, but both music and scents can remove some of that struggle, and just make the memories seem to appear out of nowhere.

In search of lost memories

In Marcel Proust's novel, *In Search of Lost Time*, a character smells a madeleine cake dipped in tea, which brings back vivid memories of his childhood rushing back. It is these memories which make up much of the book. Sure, it may just be a novel, but scents do have a powerful effect on the memory. When you smell something, it tends to connect automatically with whatever else was going on at the time for you. The smell of a flower you gave to your first love (or that was given to you) may forever stay with you, and always remind you of that every time after that you smell it. If you want to remember more about someone from the past, perhaps you could find their perfume or cologne, and this would help to stimulate your old memories.

Alphabet Method

The alphabet method is one I originally came up with to help generate creative ideas in my book *Idea Hacks*. But the interesting thing about this system is that it works quite well for finding lost memories as well. Now, let's discuss how you can use this system to retrieve lost memories.

Run through the letters of the alphabet

When you are having trouble finding a memory, go through all of the letters of the alphabet to see if any of them help to spark your memory. As an example, if you were trying to remember the name of Donald Duck, simply running through the letters A, B, C, then D, might be enough to help you remember the name. Even if all you remember is that it starts with a D, this is still information you can use as a clue to help remember the name.

If you only remember the first letter and you feel stuck, it can help to run the second letter through the full alphabet as well. For example, if you are trying to remember the country Singapore, you may remember it starts with S, and then feel stuck. You could then run the second letter through the alphabet again. Since the next letter would probably be a vowel, we could continue with those. So you could go Sa, Se, and Si may catch your attention, as we are getting closer to the word. Perhaps that would be enough to spark you to remember the country Singapore. If not, you can always continue the process for each letter until you finally do remember the full word. I will admit, this process may be a bit slow sometimes, but this should be much quicker than trying to recall a name without a system.

Logical Flow

Many people might not think logic has much to do with memory, but I find that it can help to recover a memory if you are able to figure out what logically *could* have happened, and what logically *could not* have happened. It helps to eliminate some things that could not have happened, thus making it easier for you to focus on what is more likely to have actually happened. This will help you to reconstruct the right memories.

Some simple questions you may ask yourself to try to figure out if something makes sense, are: "Does this obey the basic rules of what is typically expected in the situation?" or "Does this follow what would normally be expected for the people involved?" If something doesn't make sense, that is a strong clue that you may not be remembering it quite right.

Remember with logic and by focusing on what makes sense

Let's say you are trying to remember something about yesterday. You remember driving home from the convenience store, but you can't seem to remember what you actually picked up there. Then your mind flips to earlier in the day, and you remember your significant other was mad, yelling at you about how many necessities were missing from the house… shampoo, toothpaste, floss, and so forth. Logically, you think, you must have gone to pick up some of those items. Then, of course, the memory returns to you. Yes, you were picking up those items because you didn't want your significant other to be mad about not having them.

Here is an example of using logic and considering what makes sense, when you have arrived at a restaurant. Usually you wait a few minutes until there is an opening, they take you to your seat, then you order, then the food is delivered, after this they ask if you would like dessert, and finally you ask for the check. If for some reason you remembered something that made no sense within this order, such as the waiter offering you dessert as soon as you have a seat, then you could say that your memory doesn't make sense. In such a case, there is a decent chance you have remembered incorrectly. This may seem like a silly example, but sometimes it is easy to confuse memories from different events, which can result in such illogical memories. It is up to you to recognize these illogical memories as wrong, and to keep searching for the right ones.

Thinking through what makes sense can also help to shield you against other people's false memories. Sometimes, people misremember things. Perhaps someone tells a story about you and they get major facts wrong. You know yourself well, so you tend to notice if someone claims that you did something which you know you would never have done. A fairly safe example would be if you gave up drinking alcohol ten years ago. If someone tells a story about you drinking a lot of vodka at a recent party, you might immediately know that they are mistaken, because you no longer consume alcohol. In that case, it would be easy for you to state that this person must have a mistaken memory, as it makes no sense.

Have Conversations with Old Friends

Memories are often thought of as an individual thing that we have within ourselves, and obviously in a way they are. Our memories are stored in the brain. However, the brain interacts with the environment to form those memories. And part of our regular environment is in our social interactions. Understand that when we socialize, we will be in a better position to recall memories that we have shared with friends and family, etc.

Meet with old friends

When you meet with an old group of friends, you will begin to recall a large number of memories. You'll find that what you share are mainly your memories together, so you will likely reminisce about those old experiences. Sometimes, simply meeting with these people who represent a different era of your life, can have a similar effect as with music or with scents, where you may be brought back to the general feeling and atmosphere of that time, possibly involuntarily.

What aids these memories is also seeing each other's faces, which will act as a cue, reminding you of the things you have done together.

Reconstruct old memories together

As a group, likely some of these friends will remember certain events, and you will remember other ones. Combined, you will begin to form a full picture of the memories you shared. Contrary to what some may think, memories are not just mental photographs or videos of actual events. They are not completely perfect. Instead, memories can be more like recreations of events.

If you have ever seen a crime TV show where they perform reenactments of the events that happened, your memories are more like that than they are exact recordings of what happened. The memories are formed from your own perspective and they consider all of your prior experiences. They can be molded by your beliefs, feelings, your level of understanding, and so forth. When anyone recalls something, they are reliving it through the lens of their own worldview and expectations. This is why two people, or a group of people, may all form a different recollection of the same event. Even still, having a full group can be interesting because you can build a picture together of what your memories were.

In groups there is a power to recover lost memories, because you may recover one detail, another friend may recover another, and another friend may recover yet a different one. Combined, you will form a larger picture of these details and rebuild your memories in a more meaningful way. Of course, all of this memory recovery is only useful for the memories that you actually did share together.

Revisit Old Memories

One way to spark old memories would be if we could travel back in time and revisit some of the places we used to go to. This could be an old home, a school we attended, or simply a city we once knew. We may not be able to travel back in time, but the next best thing is to revisit the places, things, and activities that we experienced in an earlier time.

Travel to a familiar place you haven't seen in a long time

As an exercise, you may go back to a place from your early childhood and try to revive age old memories that have been long buried. If you can't literally go, travel in your mind and visualize all of the details that you possibly can. When you do this, you will tend to automatically visualize and imagine how everything used to be the last time that you were there. You may remember people, activities, or items that were there in the past.

If you are able to visit a place filled with old memories, you may recall how you felt the last time that you were there.

Or you may remember what you were doing, who else you were there with, and so forth. As you look around, you might notice that many items are similar or the same as the last time you were there. This will then spark your memories and help you remember how things used to be.

Any number of cues may help to bring back memories. You might see the same person you used to know, working in the same place. You might see, hear, or smell something that held great meaning to you. By looking around and exploring, you are more likely to come across some of these triggers, which will help recover or recreate some old memories.

Random Triggers

Sometimes no matter what you try, the memory you are after just seems too distant and foggy. You can barely pick up any of it, and so it feels like it is permanently lost. One case where this may happen is with a dream. When you have no real clues or triggers to help build up the memory, then one of the only places you can begin to recover it is with random triggers.

A random trigger just means that you seek out random ideas to get you thinking in new directions, to help trigger the correct memory. The best way to do this will be through specific websites or tools that are designed to produce pictures, icons, or words at random. A list of such resources can be found below.

Random word or picture generators

As you might imagine, it can become tedious to use random words or pictures to help recreate a memory. Obviously, you will end up with many suggestions that are completely wrong.

But if you are truly unable to make progress in finding a certain memory, a random trigger may help to provide the best path to get there.

The following are some resources that will produce random ideas, which can then help you to remember something:

- Random word generator - http://www.textfixer.com/tools/random-words.php
- Random word / icon generator - http://ideagenerator.creativitygames.net/
- Story plot idea generator - http://writers-den.pantomimepony.co.uk/writers-plot-ideas.php
- Random Wikipedia article: https://en.wikipedia.org/wiki/Special:Random
- Random quote generator: http://www.miniwebtool.com/random-quote-generator/

Reading or experiencing a wide range of information

Another way to increase your intake of random cues that might help bring back a memory, is to expose yourself to a much wider range of information. Interestingly, you may not want to spend too much time on any one source of material, but instead allow your mind to wander from topic to topic. For example, you might read article headings in various magazines, rather than read every single article thoroughly.

I actually recently had a dream that I was having trouble recalling as I awoke. As the morning went on, I read an article, and it mentioned the word "concussion", which reminded me that the dream I had was actually about a child I found, who I thought had had a concussion because he hit his head very hard. I ended up remembering more details of the dream simply because I came across that word. But I don't think I would have recovered the memory of the dream if I hadn't coincidentally come across the word "concussion". Of course, it was partly luck that I read about it in an article, but it was also more likely that I would see that word, because I read from a fairly wide range of articles and books.

The Surrounding Context

Often, the context surrounding what you are trying to remember will hold many clues to actually help you remember. Many of us focus directly on that thing which we want to remember, but it might not make much sense to focus too much on that fuzzy memory. If it isn't getting any clearer by focusing directly on what you want to remember, you may be able to look at the context to help rebuild that memory instead.

Play through surrounding events in your mind

The people who tend to remember something are usually willing to play through much of the memories that surround the event they actually want to remember. If you went to a baseball game, and later that night you went to the movie theater, but you don't recall exactly what happened in between, you could take a bit of time to play through the baseball game in your mind to see if something reminds you of what you were doing afterward. If you still aren't sure, you can play through the memories of going to the theater. There are many types of clues you might catch on to by playing through such events. One example is you might remember you and your friends wearing different clothes at the baseball game and at the movies. This could help you to remember that you actually went home and relaxed for an hour and changed clothes in between those events.

Ask What, When, Where, How, Who, and Why?

If you aren't sure where to begin, to get the full context, you can start by simply asking What, When, Where, How, Who, and Why? Answering these types of questions will help you to get a fairly strong contextual understanding of a situation. And when you know the context, you will be much more likely to remember what you are trying to recall.

As an example, perhaps you have a friend and you don't remember what her profession is. So you could ask yourself what she spends most of her time doing. Do you know where she works? Do you know what type of building she works in, at least? How does she get to work? How long has she been at this job? Who does she work for? Why does she do what she does? Answering all of these types of questions can help you to build a context around her work. It may not answer directly what work she does, but it could help you to put the puzzle pieces together and figure it out.

Admittedly, using context isn't always going to get you to the exact answer. More often than not, though, it should help you to get close. For example, perhaps when you answer all of the above questions about your friend's profession, you come to think that she is a nurse, but instead it turns out that she works as an administrative assistant at a hospital. The point is that by recreating all of the context that you can, you will build up clues and possibly remember the exact answer. But if not, at least you will be much closer than where you started.

Google it

This tip is a sort of last resort. But let's face it, sometimes you are able to remember just enough information that if you were to put it into Google, you would be able to then remember what you want. If you just want or need to get to your memory fast without struggling too much, Google can often be a useful tool. However, this isn't recommended as a first step, because the way to improve your memory is to exercise it and test it. I would recommend usually trying other techniques before going with Google.

Type your clues and triggers into Google

After going through some of the above tips, you probably have many clues and triggers that have helped you get close to recovering your memory. However, perhaps you still can't quite get it, and you just want to find it already, even if you need to "cheat" and use Google to get there.

As an example, let's say you are trying to remember Arnold Schwarzenegger's name. You've been able to remember some pretty big clues about who he is. For instance, you know that he was the actor in *The Terminator* movies, and he was a governor of California. Using Google to search for these clues would probably be enough to immediately recover his name.

Google is such a massive bank of information even typing in a few things related to what you want to remember, will often help you to locate that memory.

Avoid Losing Important Memories

Here is a system not for recalling lost memories, but to actually avoid losing memories and then needing to recall them later. Every time you lose a memory and need to recall it, you are losing time. So for certain important memories, the best thing you can do is avoid forgetting and losing them in the first place.

In certain types of work, there are a variety of tasks and projects to manage all at once. You may work on one project, then need to work some on a second project, then need to work some on a third project, and so forth. This may seem counterproductive, and you may think it would be easier to do one project at a time. However, there are many fields, such as with business people, authors, case workers, and police officers, where working on multiple projects, in different stages, is actually quite common and a necessary part of the work. Following is a key tip to help manage multiple projects and avoid forgetting.

Write notes to keep track of where you left off

The problem with working on too many jobs and tasks, all at different stages, is that it becomes easy to forget where you were, exactly. If you have subordinates and superiors that you have to manage tasks for, it may be even more important to keep track of what you have already told different people, and what stages they are at with their projects. For example, if you have instructed a subordinate to do something, you might want to make a note of it to remember to check on that later. Even if your memory is fairly good, and you can remember, there is a loss of efficiency every time you need to figure out where you left off. Time spent trying to remember is time you could have been making progress.

Keep in mind that when you put your work down, if you won't return to it for many days or a week or more, it could be worthwhile to write down a note of where you left off, or what you need to do next in regards to that project. This will help save a lot of time and trouble.

As the saying goes, "if it isn't broke, then don't fix it". So if you don't have problems managing many different projects and remembering where you left off, then this is obviously not a concern. But if you do find yourself losing time switching between projects and getting frustrated, this simple tip will allow you to effortlessly remember exactly where you were. I use this tip myself and it has been a big help in reducing frustrations. I keep notes on my actual to-do list of where I left off on different projects, so whenever I return, I can smoothly continue where I left off. My to-do list contains not just things to do, but an updated status of where any project is at any given time, and anything I am waiting for from people who work with me on those projects.

EXTERNALIZE MEMORIES

A Brief Introduction

External memories are when we use outside devices to remember things for us. They are memories that are stored outside of yourself. The upside to doing this is that you can store so much more memory externally, than you can in your brain. For example, all of the files on your computer or saved phone numbers on your phone are part of your external memory. But we have to keep in mind that this form of memory is only as good as our organizational systems are.

Much of this book has been about practicing and using your memory in order to improve it. I stand by the principle that it is critical for us to continue to exercise our memories. I believe that we should know some of the more important numbers in our lives, we should remember how to perform basic math operations by hand, and we should not rely on external memory to store *all* of our key memories. Technological failures can occur, meaning that memories and information can be lost or destroyed. Because of this, we should at least have some important information stored in our personal memories, so that we are protected against such issues.

However, there are cases where something is extremely important, and you need to remember it. If you fail to remember it, something bad will happen or you will cause yourself some great inconvenience. In such cases, I recommend taking advantage of the technological devices most of us own now, and using them to help store some external memories.

External memory tools are also important because if you want to take a practical approach to memory, as is the point of this book, then you shouldn't be trying to remember absolutely everything using your own memory. Most people I know don't want to spend all day memorizing technical documents, for example. It is more practical to remember the important things that you need to know and use. The rest, you can externalize, instead of burdening your brain with it.

The types of things you will want to consider storing in your external memory will be information that changes often, that is not important to your day to day life, or that is rather large in size.

Information that changes often might be the height or weight of a child. Information not important to your day to day life could be the speed of sound or light. And information that is rather large in size could be the digits of pi, which is actually infinite. An example that meets all three of these may be the Terms of Service for an application you use. You may read through it and understand the important points, but not actually memorize it. If you wanted to access it, it would make more sense to keep it in your external memory than to use a lot of your time committing it to your personal memory.

Use "Unforgettable Cues" to Make Sure You Remember

Do you know what an unforgettable cue would be? What would be a cue so strong that it would almost certainly help you recall the actual thing you were trying to remember? Well, it would be a cue that represents exactly what you want to recall. A cue is usually just a reminder. So, if you tie a string on your finger, it may remind you that you have to do something, but the string itself doesn't tell you exactly what you have to do. The string is a forgettable cue, because you might still forget what you are supposed to do. On the other hand, an unforgettable cue would be something that tells you exactly what you need to do. If you have an unforgettable cue, you basically cannot forget, which would be the perfect outcome for most of us. Let's go into some examples of how to find these unforgettable cues.

Don't throw away the perfect reminder

Recently I noticed that my floss container had gone empty. I was about to throw it away when I realized that needing to go to the store to buy a new container is exactly the type of thing most of us would forget. Instead of throwing away the empty and "useless" container, I decided to keep it around, so I couldn't forget that I needed to replace it. Then, I didn't just leave it in the bathroom, where it usually would be. I took it to my office, where I spend most of the day working. This is the perfect unforgettable cue, because the cue itself represents the thing I want to remember, which is just to get more floss.

Of course, you could make more of an effort to remember that you need to get the floss, perhaps visualize your teeth rotting and falling out because you didn't floss your teeth for a very long time. But for many of us, we prefer to use our brain power on important life and work concerns. Although flossing is important, it is somewhat routine and I would rather use my brain power on other things.

Prominent notes

Another form of an unforgettable cue is writing a note of what you need to remember, and leaving it in a place that you can easily see it. This way you will not need to specifically search for the note just to remember something. I often write down items on sticky notes that I don't want to clog up my memory with. They are usually things that I need to do, but not necessarily right away. I prefer to keep my concentration on my immediate tasks, so if I come up with ideas or remember other things that need to get done, I note them and move on with other more important tasks that I need to do.

Daily to-do type items are ideal to write down because these tend to shift from day to day, and it is easier and more productive to write them down instead of truly memorizing them. Since they change often, you would always be in the process of memorizing them, which may not be the most practical use of your memory. If I memorize something, I prefer for it to be something that will *not* change, such as an actual fact. Of course, even facts change occasionally. This is because science and progress sometimes reveals that the things we thought we knew, were actually incorrect. But generally, facts are more stable than something like a to-do item.

As a quick story, I once saw a graduate student who had a very important meeting he had to attend, that he needed to make sure he would not forget. Apparently, he had missed an important meeting in the past, so he decided to take actions to stop his forgetfulness. What he did was take a large sticky note and attach it to his computer monitor where it actually obstructed a chunk of the screen. But he left it there because he simply could not forget that it was there, since it constantly annoyed him (by blocking the screen). This may be a bit unusual, but at least he didn't miss his meetings anymore.

Set an alarm

When you have something that needs to be done at a specific time, setting an alarm can be helpful. Many phones even let you note the exact event you are setting the alarm for, if you are worried that you might forget why the alarm rang. Whether you have an event that is rare, and that you worry you will forget, or whether you have a task you need to do often at regular time intervals, such as take medication, setting an alarm can help to make sure that you remember them. Rare events are easy to forget because we don't usually do them. And common events are also easy to forget because we do them often and they lose their sense of importance.

I would trust an alarm more than I would trust asking someone to remind you. Often, the person you ask to remind you will forget, because what you want them to remember probably isn't something that is very relevant to them. If it doesn't affect their life, it is much easier for them to forget it. And anyway, we should take personal accountability for the things that we need to remember.

As a word of caution about alarms, you need to make sure you have the alarm on you, or when it rings you will probably not hear it. For example, your alarm may be on a watch or a phone that you always carry.

Take a picture

For things such as remembering the exact spot in a parking garage that you parked the car, you could take a photo of the sign identifying the area. Or perhaps you are shopping for an expensive item such as a big flat screen TV, and you want to take note of the model numbers so you can research them at home and make the best choice. Rather than stand around memorizing model numbers, it probably makes more sense to take a snapshot of the ones that you want to recall, so you can research them later.

Another time you might want to take a photo is when there is a scene that you want to reflect on later to fully appreciate it. However, unless you have a specific need to remember a scene, taking too many photos is not necessarily good for your memory. Dr. Linda Henkel from Fairfield University has found that the more pictures we take, the less we actually tend to remember. She has said:

> "People so often whip out their cameras almost mindlessly to capture a moment, to the point that they are missing what is happening right in front of them."

It seems that we come to over-rely on the pictures to store our memories for us. Also, if you are worried about taking photos, you may be paying less attention to what is actually happening around you, reducing your ability to remember overall. Therefore, I would recommend to take few photos when the scenery is beautiful, and instead to focus on enjoying the moment.

Send Yourself a Reminder

For many people, sending a reminder to yourself can help to remember some of those important things that need to get done. Part of using these tips effectively is knowing yourself. If you often check your emails or text messages and take action on them, this could be a great way to remember something you need to do.

Write yourself a text or email reminder

Although this is similar to writing sticky notes to yourself, I consider it different because some people will have more success with one way or another.

Most of us use email and smart phones at this point, so why not use these readily available tools? This tip can be more useful for short-term things you want to remember. For instance, if you send yourself a text, you will obviously get it right away. So the next time you check your phone, you will remember that you need to perform a task when you see that text. This works similarly with emails. Personally, I get enough emails that I will probably only pay attention to the ones that come in within about the prior 24 hours. So if I send myself a message, I should plan to act on it within that period, or take the risk of the email getting pushed down with the older ones until I forget about it.

Another way to use this tip is to send the email or text to someone else who perhaps could also use the information. This will just help to reinforce the memory, and make it less likely that you both would forget about it. For example, if you are going on a trip with your significant other and you want to remember to look up some of the top tourist destinations, then you could send an email reminder to your significant other. You can send it to yourself too, to reduce the chances of both of you forgetting.

Keep a Log of Important Events

In time, without constant review, it's easy to forget things. You can train your memory to improve using the tactics in this book, but it is unrealistic to expect to remember everything going back weeks, months, and years. It probably makes more sense to actually record some parts of your life. Some memorable times you may wish to record are if you are recently married, if you have young children, or if you have been hired to do your dream job.

Keep a notebook (online or offline) to record important events

Recording events in a notebook is a good way to remember the details of what happens in your life. As time passes, it is easy to forget the day to day occurrences, but with a notebook you can keep them much longer.

I do keep a regular journal, but instead of documenting what happens to me, I tend to record lessons I am learning, or things I think I could change to improve something in my life. Rather than documenting events, I tend to record my thought processes. This is interesting because in time I can see if my thoughts and understanding are improving. If I am getting worse in some way, I can pay more attention to that and make an effort to improve in that area.

With the memories of the details of our lives, we can either acknowledge that many of them will be lost in time, or we can specifically make an effort to record some of them. Of course, you can do this through not just notebooks, but also through video, photos, or audio recordings. When you keep track of your progress in some way, you will see patterns and learn, helping you to avoid repeating the same mistakes.

Protocols and Systems

Sometimes, there are many steps that you need to take in order to accomplish something. And perhaps you only need to perform this action every once in a while, so it is easy to forget the steps, or in what sequence you need to do them. This can be aggravating of course, but there is a way to help overcome such problems.

Building protocols and systems tends to make more sense to serve as a reminder of how to deal with these types of tasks. As an example, the task may be to do your taxes, things to remember before you go on a flight, the long distance area codes to dial family in different places, and so forth. If you externalize these memories, then you can be much better prepared when you need them.

Make a checklist

The easiest way to use your external memory to remember exactly what you need to do is to build checklists that have all of your steps in the order that you need to accomplish them. Even if you have a very good memory, it is often better to use a checklist for either tasks that you do rarely and often forget a few steps, or for tasks where making any mistake or forgetting any one step will cause big problems for you. Otherwise, you may need to re-learn how to do a task every time you need to do it, which is inefficient and a big nuisance. Or worse, you may risk making a big mistake if you misremember what you needed to do.

The trick with this is to recognize the types of tasks that always give you some difficulty in remembering them. When you are struggling to remember a process, and it causes you a lot of frustration, this is probably a great task to build a checklist for. It may be easier to create these checklists while you are actually doing the task. If you try to make the checklist at another time, you are likely to forget some key steps. In time, you will learn to recognize the types of tasks which are ideal for making checklists, and you will do this before the task becomes a frustrating problem for you.

Keep in mind that it is best to be very specific with the steps you take. For example, if part of your steps involve logging into an account that you rarely use, you may want to include your login and password in the steps. Otherwise, when you try to do this and time has passed, you are likely to have forgotten that detail. Be very cautious of assuming that you will remember even minor steps. I prefer to go into detail on every step that needs to be accomplished.

The Internet itself

Our greatest source of external memories that we use every day is in the internet itself. You may not think of this as memory, and perhaps it isn't a collection of your personal memories. But if you think of it, the internet is a collection of the memories of all of humanity. Isn't that even better?

Wikipedia

Wikipedia can be used to remember anything you need to know about almost any topic. While some are suspicious that anyone can alter the contents of Wikipedia, in practice, the information is usually quite accurate. One of the best features about Wikipedia is that its content is always adapting. Again, some may be suspicious of changing content, but as our world changes and adapts, so does the information we know. Wikipedia gets updated all of the time in order to adjust to the new information we have.

If you know that Wikipedia is always available, you don't necessarily need to try to memorize everything about a given topic. Instead, you can use the site as a reference and check on the information when you need to use it, or when you need to know it.

Google it

There are so many sites being added to the internet every day, that it is impossible to keep up with them all. Nonetheless, instead of needing to memorize every detail or every fact about everything, you can always simply use Google or other internet sites to recall or learn specific information when you need it.

Keep in mind that if you want to be sure that you are accessing the most up to date information, then you can always go to Settings > Advanced Search, and under "Last Update", you can select to see searches only from the past 24 hours, the past week, month, or year. For information that changes rapidly, such as advice on hot stocks to invest in, you will probably want to use this feature.

Use Searchable Systems

A huge benefit of systems where you can keep an external memory, is that often they are searchable. This means you can quickly search for the exact information or memory that you want to retrieve, kind of like you would with Google.

It is difficult to overstate just how much time and energy you can save yourself with searchable systems. To give you a comparison, imagine if I were to hand you a 1,000+ page book such as "War and Peace", and I asked you to find a specific quote for me. This would take you quite a long time. Most people would probably get frustrated and quit. On the other hand, if you have the book in PDF or some digital form, you can simply have the computer search the file for the quote, and pull it up in a matter of seconds.

The more memories and information you store externally, the more important it will be that it is not only organized, but searchable.

Try Evernote

As far as external memory tools or programs go, I highly recommend Evernote. It is a free application where you can keep notebooks and notes organized as you wish using cloud storage. That means you should be safe from losing any information you put on there. Regardless of whether you use Evernote or not, a key benefit of this particular program is that you can search your memories. This is a huge benefit, because it means even if your organization isn't the best, you can still locate your memories quickly.

"Ctrl + F" is usually the fastest way to search

Whether you are in Evernote, in a Microsoft Word file, in a PDF, or on a random website on the internet, try using Ctrl + F (hitting both the Ctrl and the F keys on your keyboard) and searching for exactly what you are looking for.

Let's say you use Evernote and you keep a personal journal there, writing a page every day for 10 years. At the end, you have about 3,650 pages of your personal life in there. If you want to review some days where you were your happiest, to remember them, you could search through all of your entries page by page. However, it would be more efficient to simply hit Ctrl + F, and search for "happy", or "happiness". Actually, I would just search for "happ" because this will include both of those words in the results.

The bottom line is that there is no need to spend too much time looking for a memory in the modern digital age. Use a service that can find it for you instantly.

GEOGRAPHICAL & TRAVEL MEMORIES

A Brief Introduction

This section is more specific than the others, in that it isn't just about general types of memories, but specifically about your memory when traveling to new places, or even when you go on new paths within a familiar city.

This is a section I wanted to include for a couple of reasons. One is that I do like to travel, but my geographical and travel memories have been a weak point for me. However, I have noticed much improvement in my ability to remember during travel with memory tips such as the ones included here.

The other reason I wanted to include this section is because I think geographical memories are very important. I have occasionally heard stories of someone taking a wrong turn somewhere, either in the woods or during a big storm, and getting completely lost to the point of having an emergency situation. The results are sometimes tragic and in the worst cases people have lost their lives. It can be a big danger to get lost, of course, but it can also be a big inconvenience in general.

I am sure many people will say that it's easy to use GPS, so why bother with geographical memories? It's true that GPS can be a helpful tool. I think it is useful for finding nearby restaurants or places of interest, or to help navigate a new route. But do you want to be looking down at your GPS all of the time while you're walking in a new and exciting place, or do you want to enjoy the site seeing? Also, the more your eyes are fixated on a screen, the less you are picking up of the scenery, making it even less likely that you will actually remember your environment.

As a side story about GPS, I personally knew someone who lived in a medium sized city for three years and who still needed her GPS to get to common locations, such as stores, friends' homes, etc. She was a Ph.D. student, so lack of intelligence was not the issue. It was just a bad habit of relying so much on the GPS that she never really learned or remembered the city.

Now, I'm going to start us off with two basic tips that you need to know.

Travel during the day

It's best to travel in the day when you visit an unknown place. In the night, you cannot see well, which will make it difficult to remember later on. Also, you may end up somewhere unsafe, making it uncomfortable to stop and ask for directions. However, you might choose to make an exception if you already know that an area is well lit, well populated, and relatively safe in the night time. Without this knowledge, however, you may be taking a risk to explore at that time.

Go alone or lead

You should either be alone or leading someone else when trying to build up your memory power for navigating. If you are just following someone else, it is easy to become too reliant on them for directions, making your mind become lazy, where you will be more likely to forget the layout of the area. At first, I recommend traveling on your own. When you get a basic sense of confidence, then you can lead someone else around, starting with the areas you are familiar with. Then, after you have gained ability and confidence in your travels, you can try leading another person on path that is new and unfamiliar to the both of you.

Know Some Basic Facts of Navigation and Travel

You will want to learn some basic facts about traveling to help you stay oriented. When you can understand certain patterns and trends, and have a basic knowledge of navigation, this will help you to know where you are, and avoid getting lost. Or if you do get lost, it will not be for as long as it might have been if you did not have this knowledge.

Maps

As soon as you can, I recommend getting a town or city level map of the area you are visiting. This will help to give you an overview of the area. You might notice patterns, such as places where there are more shops or tourist destinations. This will help you plan out your trip.

When you have your map, make note of the cardinal directions, key symbols, the scale of the map, and what area it covers. These are basic features you will need to read it.

Even if you don't think you will need to use a map very much, it can be a useful tool to have just in case you get lost or disoriented. You can always use the map to figure out where you are, and then find a path to get to your desired location.

To figure out where you are, search for nearby landmarks or major streets in the real world, then find them on your map. When you have located a few landmarks or streets, this should be enough to help you position your map to face the same way that you are looking (e.g., to make it so you are looking north, and the map is also facing north). From there, it should be easy to find nearby locations you wish to go to.

If you are concerned about your map reading skills, I recommend getting a local map of where you live, and using it to help you explore your own town before you travel somewhere new.

Cardinal directions

It is always helpful to have some idea of where your cardinal directions are – north, south, east, and west. If you have an idea of which general direction you are headed, and which general direction you need to go to return to where you started, this can help make your journey much easier. The other key reason you want to know cardinal directions is that it will make reading maps simpler. Knowing that everything has a relative position to everything else, whether north of it, east of it, etc., is easier for you to understand than to think that everything is located in a random direction.

One big clue is the sun. It always rises in the east, and sets in the west. For the night time, it can help to learn some key star clusters, such as the Big Dipper and the North Star, to help you find north even if the sun is not up. Also, keep in mind that many smartphones have a compass app as well, or you can simply purchase a compass to help navigate. I recommend owning a compass of some sort. If you have trouble orienting your map so it faces the same way you are facing, a compass makes this much easier too. Just make it so north on the map is pointing the same way as north points on your compass (or you can choose any other direction you wish).

A key feature you must realize about the cardinal directions is that you only need to know one, and then you know them all. Everyone probably understands that south is opposite to north, and east is opposite to west. But another thing to realize is that if you know north, then east will always be 90 degrees to the right, and west will always be 90 degrees to the left. If you see the sun is just rising in the east, then north is 90 degrees to the left of that. Understand that by knowing one cardinal direction, you can figure them all out easily.

Know Your Position Compared to Key Points

The most common key points you will come across are landmarks. You should always keep an eye out for key landmarks that you can use to help guide your way. These could be parks, special libraries, museums, especially tall buildings, monuments, statues, cathedrals, fountains, or homes or buildings dedicated to famous or significant people. Landmarks are just places that catch your attention.

Wherever you are, keep a running track record of landmarks and their relation to each other. If you get confused or easily lost, make sure to carry a map to keep the relationships between different key areas in mind.

Know your starting point

When you are arriving somewhere new, you should pay special attention, as you will need to remember how to leave when it is time to go. It's usually easy to enter a new area. There may be signs all leading toward the place you want to go. But when it is time to leave, people may need to go in different directions, so there are not always signs telling you exactly where to go to leave. In case there are no signs, you should at least remember the path you took to arrive, as you might be able to use that same path to leave.

Even if you've just been dropped off by a bus in a new area, don't undermine the importance of remembering your drop off point. Chances are the bus will come back to the same area to pick you up, so you have to develop a good memory for where you arrived. Make a note of several significant things in the area, not just the obvious fact that it is a bus stop. If you get lost and ask someone about a bus stop, it may turn out that there are a large amount of bus stops, for different types of buses, all over the area. This starting point is so important that you might even take a few photos of the area, if you aren't fully confident that you'll remember how to get back. In the worst case, you can ask someone if they know how to get to the location of the photos.

Other key points and landmarks

As mentioned above, you should always have an idea of your starting point, since you will need to eventually go back. But sometimes we travel farther and farther away from that location, and it makes sense to develop other points of reference along the way. When I travel with people, often they are excited to get to know a new area, and we can easily walk miles away from our starting point.

But you may quickly find that you've taken many side streets, and that you have lost track of your starting point. The key here is to build new reference points, and to remember where you are in comparison to that.

When traveling, everywhere is a new place, and you will always be lost if you are not keeping in mind where you are in reference to a known place. If you don't know where you are right now, or where you are in reference to a known point, then you are lost. It is that simple. So when traveling, the objective is to avoid having this happen. Your starting point is the most important reference point, but it will be very helpful to establish more along the way, as you get to know a new area.

Periodically, you will want to stop in key areas, such as landmarks, or areas with many landmarks, and build a mental picture of such places. You should also stop and think about how these places relate to other major points or landmarks that you know. As a side note, if you are in an area loaded with landmarks, choose a few special places to build as reference points in your mind. Everything can't be a reference point for you, or that will mean you are trying to remember everything, which is a mistake.

Remember the Path to Return Where You Came From

I have noticed that some people can see a path from one direction, and they may automatically build a mental map of the area so that they can navigate it easily even if they were walking the opposite way. I'm not one of those people. A path that looks similar walking in one direction, will look different to me, walking it in the opposite direction. But of course, usually when you walk in one direction, you intend to return along that path to get back to your original point. So it's important to build a solid understanding of both ways of travel.

What would stand out on your return?

Keep in mind any important parts of the scenery that will stand out to you when you are returning along a path. First of all, it will be important to note any shops, buildings, or anything else on corners where you changed direction. If you are traveling straight on a path, and that leads you to your destination, then there isn't much to remember. However, that is rare. If you have to turn a corner occasionally, you will want to pay special attention to what is on those corners. Remember to be more attentive to less common places and stores, because if they are too common, you will see them everywhere and so it won't be a helpful memory aid.

Through your travels, you will begin to learn what types of details you are better at remembering. Is it the corner shops, the street names, or landmarks? If you have a specific strength, you can use it to your advantage and pay more attention to that. In general though, you should pay enough attention to your environment to sense if you take a wrong turn and go down the wrong path. You would sense this because there would be nothing on the street that is familiar. Through paying attention and building memories, you will have certain expectations, so if none of that is there, you know you are in the wrong place.

The Changing Environment

As we have established, you should not try to remember everything, since that is counterproductive. One of the things you should not bother trying to remember is that which will tend to change often in your environment. This is because if something is there one moment, and it changes the next, this will confuse your memory. It is better to know that certain things will be likely to change, so that you can ignore them and focus on what is more stable and worth remembering.

Don't remember the things that change

Some things that might change and move are a hot dog stand on wheels, a blue parked car, or clothing hanging on a clothesline. All of these things will easily change in the course of a day. So if you pick one of them to remember to help you learn a new location, then you will be left confused when they have been moved. Other things that you don't want to focus on remembering are groups of people. Even if there is a party or some kind of a rally going on and there are a lot of people, they can easily go away or move somewhere else, meaning it won't help you to use them as a sort of landmark.

Remember the things that are permanent

The permanent features are the ones that are worth remembering. For example, when going to a new friend's home, you may remember that there is a 4-way stop with a red-flashing light intersection. This is unlikely to get moved or changed suddenly, so it is a good feature to remember. Or you may remember that in an area with a variety of trees, that there is one willow tree that looks different from all the other ones. The willow is a tree with a unique type of leaf that hangs down, making it stand out. Obviously trees do not usually move, and there is no reason to think this one would get chopped down anytime soon, making it a useful landmark to remember.

Remember the Rare Things

Remember the things that have some rarity, and are not so common as to be found everywhere. For example, you will be better off remembering that there is a community bank with a unique name on a given street, instead of remembering that it had a Starbucks on it. If you only remembered the Starbucks, then you would be likely to confuse yourself later on when you see Starbucks on many different streets. As another example, it will also be better to remember a uniquely painted mural on a wall rather than a satellite dish that seems to be on many households in an area.

Have a general idea of common store and restaurant chains in the area

Many places around the world now have Starbucks, McDonalds, and certain convenience stores, banks, and pharmacies will probably be common depending on where you are. These are the types of places that can be found again and again, and they are often so common that using them as a memory aid can be a big mistake. In some cases, a chain is common enough that it can be found on most streets in the area, making it very confusing if you tried to use it as a reference point.

As you travel, it is important to pay attention to what the common elements are that you see everywhere, and what types of places or things are rarer. You have to get used to the structure of things in your new area, because the assumption or patterns from where you came from could be completely different in this new place. Things that are strange and different to you may be quite common in this new place. And things that are common to you may be quite rare here. For you to use something as a memory aid, it needs to be rare in the area. Whether it is rare or unusual in your hometown will not matter. Keep the context in mind.

Rare things to remember

An antique ornamental bike that is outside of an antique shop is more memorable than a shop that has yo-yos outside of it, in an area where many shops have the same exact yo-yos set out in the same way. Also, perhaps a place has a unique sounding name that catches your attention. This could be worth remembering. Another way a place can be rare is by the type of function or service that it provides. Maybe you see a restaurant that serves only one type of dish, but it is so good that there is a long line of customers. That seems uncommon enough to be worth remembering. You want to build up memories for these "one of a kind" type places or features that when you remember them, it is a valuable memory because it isn't something that can be confused with a bunch of other places.

Be Willing to Explore New Areas

When you are getting to know a new area, you will probably only know a few places well. For that reason, it is more important to stretch beyond what you know, so you can begin to learn new areas. Learning how different places interconnect is good not just for building new memories, but will help you be much more efficient in your travels as well.

Venture beyond the areas you know

It is a mistake to always travel in the same ways to the same places. For instance, when visiting a new city, state, or country, you may take a bus to get to one part of the city, and then another part, and another part. You would stop in different areas and build an understanding of these disconnected parts of the city.

As you get more comfortable with the new environment, it may make more sense to venture on your own beyond those closed areas that you have already visited.

Perhaps you have learned many different areas and you know them well, but you don't know how they interconnect. If you insist on always staying within the areas you already know, you may end up wasting a lot of time, taking a much longer route than needed, when there was a much shorter path available. Instead, by venturing beyond what you know, you will expand your mental map of the area. You will need to stay focused to be sure to remember any new places you go to, and how they connect with the places you are already familiar with. Again, it will be best to explore new areas well before night time.

Look for shortcuts

After you've gained some familiarity with an area, this will be a good time to try out shortcuts. You don't want to become too complacent in taking the same roads and paths all of the time. You should pay attention to roads that seem to connect to where you want to go, even if they are unfamiliar. Of course, you will need to learn to recognize which paths may be dead ends. In general, if the streets are very small or if there are no stores or shops on them, or if it simply has the appearance of a residential neighborhood, then it may not interconnect well with other areas. If you are concerned with taking a dead end street, then you might use a tool like Google Maps to help see if the paths interconnect or not. Otherwise, you might simply ask a passerby for help.

What is this Place?

How many buildings or places have you passed by, and had no idea what their purpose was. If you live in a city, or visit a city, there are so many buildings that it can just become a great big blur in the background. However, remember that part of memory is based on understanding. If you have no understanding of the significance of the places around you, everything will seem to have no real pattern or order. And therefore, you will not have a great memory for these places.

Figure out the purpose of a place

As you pass by all types of buildings, if you have no idea what they are for, slow down a bit and try to figure it out. For example, someone from the US who visits Mexico may notice a pattern of seeing names like Banamex and Santander. But in the US, these names are not recognized. Seeing them in many places in Mexico though, it would make sense to learn what these buildings are about. Actually, they are the names of specific banks. Of course, if you are traveling to a new land, it is a good idea to learn about such names common to the area, which may not be common where you came from.

Keep in mind that all kinds of places have names that don't give you much of any idea of what they are about. So you may find yourself traveling in an area with many buildings which you have no real idea what their purpose is. You may feel lost even when traveling in your hometown, because many of us never actually stop to ask what the purpose of a building may be. This may seem silly, but learning these things will give you extra information that will make it much less likely for you to forget the building or its location. This then helps you to remember anything else close to the area. You might simply choose to enter a place and look around for clues as to what the building is about, or you could ask someone inside.

What do You Feel?

When traveling, or doing anything, often there is a feeling that we get about what we experience. Is it good, bad, funny, happy, sad, sentimental, or exciting? There are so many feelings and emotions we may have, and focusing on these can help us to have one more thing to cue a memory with.

The late poet Maya Angelou has said "I've learned that people will forget what you said, people will forget what you did, but people will never forget how you made them feel." This is often true, and what she says goes to show just how important feelings are for our memories. We tend to remember the way people or things make us feel.

Get in touch with your feelings

Some people have intense feelings about much of the things they experience, and this tends to be a tool they can use automatically in remembering locations, or anything else. In being so attuned to their feelings, they can often remember how they felt at certain times, and what made them feel that way. To use this as a tip, it may help to ask yourself more often about how you are feeling, and why. For example, in your travels you could ask: "How does what I see make me feel?"

As an example of how the feeling person might experience their travels, imagine this. The exquisite ornaments you see as you pass a shop may make you feel in awe of the craftsmanship, then passing by an alleyway of angry people yelling may make you feel scared, and then you may be very happy to see and taste ice cream from an ice cream shop, delighting in the smells and flavors. If you are not normally very in tune with what exactly you are feeling, paying special attention to them can help sense them more fully, which can help to remember more.

Embellish the feelings

If your feelings about your environment are generally mild, choosing to exaggerate them in your mind can help as a memory aid. For example, if you have a mild distaste for the color yellow and you see a yellow house as you are walking down the street, you may tell yourself that you hate the way it looks, and you could imagine a bull dozer knocking the house down. This of course would just be an exaggeration to use as a memory aid, and not an actual wish. You'll be much more likely to remember something based on a vivid or exaggerated feeling than you would a mild one.

Spend More Time at Major Centers

Occasionally in your travels, there will be a major center. I don't have an exact definition for this, as these major areas will have different features depending on where you go. But to give you an idea, a major center may contain especially large and important buildings. It may be an area where many people are gathered and clearly there is much more to see, do, and experience. Likely, it will be a place where many other paths are leading into it, or where there are many signs pointing to its location. It will pay off to spend more time in these places, remembering them in greater detail.

Take a mental picture

As they say, "a picture is worth a thousand words". It's helpful to take a mental picture of major centers, streets, landmarks, special locations, etc. Stop and take the time to observe these central areas in more detail, and not just pass through them like if they were just any other place. This area will be especially important to remember, and you will want to think about how it connects to other important landmarks or locations you are familiar with.

Learn the paths that lead in and out of the center

Occasionally in your travels, there will be a major center area, where all roads seem to lead to that place. In Spain, for example, Puerta del Sol (Gate of the Sun) has many paths leading to a central area. One notable feature is a famous bronze statue of a bear and strawberry tree in the area. If you are adventurous, you may want to visit all of the paths outward for at least a short while, to learn what is nearby.

Exploring beyond the center itself will only help you to further build your memories and understanding of the area.

Focus Your Attention Outward Instead of Inward

In order to remember new things, recall the importance of attention. If you aren't paying much attention to your surroundings, but instead to thoughts that deal with something else, then you might remember your thoughts, but not the surroundings. Or if your attention goes to conversations that don't relate to the environment and new locations, you might have the same problem. Therefore, it is important to keep your attention directed on your surroundings, and on what you wish to remember.

Watch what you talk about

If you travel in a group, as we are social creatures, you may be inclined to talk about a variety of topics. However, to keep your mind on the scenery, locations, and surroundings, you may want to avoid talking too much, or at least avoid getting too involved in deep conversations. Personally, I struggle to think about a detailed conversation I'm having, and remembering a new unfamiliar area all at the same time. I imagine many other people do as well.

Of course, many people love to talk and it will not be easy to avoid talking for a full group. My recommendation there is to keep most of your conversational topics on the setting, scenery, your impressions, and feelings, but to generally relate most of your talk to the new things that you are experiencing. The point is to try to avoid going off in too many other directions that take you away from the moment. If you do this, at the end of the day you will remember much more of the experience.

Have a Backup Plan

This is a book on memory, but given that we are talking about traveling to new areas, I feel it is important that you have backup plans to help you find where you need to go, in case you do get lost. No one wants to get lost, and many of us never plan to get lost, but we should still be prepared for the possibility. The following are items or resources that will help you if this should happen.

Phone

You should keep a phone so you can call anyone else you have been traveling with. Of course, be sure that you have their phone numbers stored. Possibly, they can help you to get directions. Keep in mind that if they have a computer and the internet, they could use GPS to help you navigate while you talk to them.

You should also be prepared in case your phone runs out of batteries. The best thing to do would be to memorize the phone numbers of at least a couple of people that you are traveling with, so you could contact them with someone else's phone or through a pay phone if necessary.

It would also make sense to know the number for the police in your area. If it is late and you feel unsafe, they may be able to help you get to your destination. Also, the number for a taxi service could help, as they would likely know how to find you and pick you up, so you could get home. Of course, you will need to have some cash to pay for the service.

GPS

Although GPS is an important tool, I also think it is important not to rely on it too much. If every time you leave a building to go somewhere, you pull out your GPS, your navigational skills will never improve. For general use, I think it is fine to use it to help show you places of interest. But I wouldn't rely on it too often. Instead of keeping your GPS open at all times, you might test your memory by viewing how to get somewhere, then trying to get there without watching the screen all of the time.

Of course, there is always the chance that you do get lost and lose track of how to return to a familiar place. In that case, the most efficient way to proceed would be to use GPS.

Compass and Map

As a quick reminder, you should also have a map and a compass in case your GPS runs out of batteries or malfunctions. A compass will be helpful if you know the general direction that you need to go in.

A map should also be useful if you are lost, but of course you will need to find your location on the map for it to help. Somehow this is the type of thing I, and everyone I know always forget to bring on a trip. Luckily, even if you forget, you can usually buy one at many convenience shops.

Simply ask

Of course, you can always just stop and ask someone for help. In my experience, this gets very mixed results, and requires some caution. Often, people are actually eager to help. But the problem with this is they can easily lead you in the wrong direction, even if it is unintentional. If they know the area very well, then everything is obvious to them. When things are obvious, they often forget to mention certain details. So they may forget to tell you something very important, because to them it was obvious. For example, they could say you need to take a right onto the bridge, but fail to mention that to do this you actually need to go left and circle around to then turn right.

Even if the person doesn't know the area well, they may try to help anyway. The problem is since they aren't very knowledgeable, they are likely to tell you something wrong, and get you more lost than you already were.

If you do find yourself asking for directions, be willing to ask more than just one person. As you think you are getting closer to your destination, continue to ask people if the place you are going to is nearby. Do not rely too much on any one person for directions, as they can often be mistaken.

Also, it helps to know larger landmarks next to your destination. Perhaps you are simply headed to a small hotel that most locals do not know. But if your hotel is next to a major landmark, most people should be able to tell you the general direction you need to go in.

CONCLUDING THOUGHTS

"Memory training is not just for the sake of performing party tricks; it's about nurturing something profoundly and essentially human."

—Joshua Foer

In this section, there will be a brief review of some of the most important points in this book. These are the takeaway points I want you to leave with. Of course, if you want to apply a specific tip from the book, I would recommend going back and reviewing it when you want to apply it.

Work on Your Mental and Physical Well-Being

At the beginning of this book, I mentioned that at one point I had problems with attention, sleep, eating, and stress. I believe the mind needs to be fairly clear so you can pay attention to new things and build those memories. With too many issues of this type, strategies to improve your memory will have limited effects. If you feel that such issues are holding you back, you can always make efforts to improve upon them, or if they are too severe, you may consult a professional for extra help.

You also want to have a decent diet, as you are made up of the things that you put into your body. I am not qualified in nutrition or diet, but many of the foods we eat will impact brain functioning. The ones that impact your general health are also highly important, as if you are not healthy, then your mind will tend to be distracted with that. Given this, it is pretty clear to me that you will want to have a solid diet with good nutrition. Personally, I strive to eat more natural foods, fruits and vegetables, less junk or processed foods, and less sugar. If you are concerned about your diet and its possible effects on your memory, I recommend consulting your physician or a dietician.

Before You Blame Your Memory…

Many years ago when I suffered with a poor memory, it took me a while to realize that memory wasn't actually the issue. It was my attention that had a severe problem. Without paying attention, you will not be able to build strong new memories.

Attention is very important, but it turns out that there are actually four things you need to have in order to build strong memories: attention, intention, organization, and understanding.

With attention, you focus enough on something to experience it fully. If your mind is elsewhere, there is no way to really remember, because you never fully experienced it.

With intention, you plan to remember. You decide something is important enough that you will remember it. We are surrounded by countless amounts of information. Without a plan to remember something, you are pretty likely to forget it, or never fully experience and attend to it in the first place.

With organization, you will have a structure to information, which allows you to remember it. Without organization, you will lack understanding, and ultimately the information will be easily forgotten.

Organization is often what helps you to build a higher level of understanding. When you understand, you can then build new memories much more easily on top of old ones. To lack understanding means that all new information doesn't seem to fit along with anything else, which makes it so much more difficult to remember.

Is It Important That I Remember This with My Own Brain?

This may seem like a silly question, but we live in an age where you can use external memories, and remember things without storing them in your brain. Practically speaking, whether information is in your computer where you can retrieve it in two seconds, or whether it is in your brain may not matter. You have to decide what is worth storing in your brain, and what is worth storing externally.

If we are speaking about memories that relate to your work, that people expect you to know, then yes, you need to remember that with your own brain. If we are speaking of a routine process you have to do once a year, which you often forget about, then I don't believe you need to stress over committing that to memory. Perhaps making a checklist of how to do it would suit you better, externalizing that memory.

In the practical world, you should ask yourself if it is important that you remember something with your own brain. If not, give yourself a break and store it externally.

Focus on Your Weaknesses and Biggest Problems

You don't need to have a perfect memory, and there is no such thing anyway. I believe when it comes to memory, you want it to be good enough in many different areas. Your memory may be better for some things than others. Pay attention, and whichever areas present you with the most problems are the ones you should focus more on, to strengthen those weak points.

One of my weak areas is navigation and travel memory. Part of the reason for this is that my mind wanders a lot to other things. This is something I have had to work on, to keep focused on the setting. Keep in mind that at one point, most of the memory tips in this book were foreign even to me. One thing that helped me is when a friend revealed a big problem I had with learning locations. He said I was trying to remember everything, which was a big mistake. Instead, I needed to remember certain key places. It was more important to know *what* to remember, than to actually have a better memory. Understanding this one key weakness, and working on it, helped improve my ability to remember locations immediately.

When you have big weaknesses, it is easy to become overwhelmed, which is bad for memory. If you find yourself getting overwhelmed by your weaknesses, I recommend previewing or pre-learning, which means exposing yourself to what you want to remember, but beforehand. If you want to remember a lecture, preview the material in the book before class. Also, for your weak areas, you should spend some time reviewing those memories after you've learned them, to try to make sure you remember them in the long-term. For example, if you just traveled to a new city and returned home, you could spend some time reviewing your memories mentally even when you're back home.

Dig Deeper

If you really want to remember something, don't give up too easily. I have noticed a pattern in the people I know with the best memories. You might think their memories are so great that they do not struggle to remember, because it is just easy for them. However, I've noticed that they do struggle just as much as anyone else. In fact, I think it is likely that they struggle *more*. When they have trouble remembering something, they do not give up on it. They tend to continue to search and search, until they find it. Also, they rarely rely on Google or other tools to "cheat" and find the memory. Another interesting thing I've noticed is that it disturbs them when they can't remember something. This is probably one of the reasons they feel compelled to keep searching for the memory, to ease the tension.

I'm sure it is often the case that we feel we have forgotten something, but part of the issue is that we do not put much effort into finding the memory. Perhaps we are just assuming we have forgotten, but really it is still within us somewhere, just buried deep. I believe if we committed to digging deeper, we would find much more memories inside of us than we thought we actually had.

Know Your Limitations

Some people can naturally process a massive amount of information in a very short time. If you cannot do this, do not worry. The way to maximize your memory is to know your limits. If you begin to feel overwhelmed when you try to remember more than a certain amount of information, then perhaps you should plan to take a break when that happens.

Cramming for exams may be useful for remembering in the short-term, but horrible for remembering information in the long-term. Give yourself a break after a certain point, if you have been using your memory a lot in a given day. Sometimes, if there is a lot of information, and you don't have the option to slow things down or take a break, the best move will probably be to identify the most important things, and just focus on remembering that and nothing else.

Review Your Memories

Many of us probably think of memories as a sort of on/off switch. Either you have the memory, or you don't. But this is only partly true. For long-term memories that are very well established, they do tend to be either on or off. However, your shorter-term or mid-term memories are in more of a gray area, where if you don't use them or review them in some way, in time you are likely to lose those memories. For this reason, if a memory is very important to you, it is critical to give it extra attention. You can't assume that just because you are able to recall something once that this means it is permanently stored. You should identify your important memories first, and then proceed to use the following tips to review them so you can start a path to retain them for the long-term.

Some of the best ways to review memories may involve: testing yourself, teaching what you learn to someone else, organizing and reorganizing information, and reviewing prior recorded thoughts or journal entries. You can review things mentally, just going through it in your mind, or you can use physical aids such as objects that remind you of something.

For example, I keep notes on the books that I read so I

can remember what I read in greater detail. Instead of just taking notes and forgetting about them, I purposely take some time to occasionally review them. This helps me to make sure I retain the most important knowledge from the books I have read. Without taking such notes and reviewing them, it is easy to forget a book in the long-term.

Study People with Strong Memories in Your Daily Life

Perhaps you are thinking "I learned some useful things in this book, but how do I keep learning more practical memory tips from here on?" And I would tell you, do what I did in the creation of this book. All I did was spend years of my life paying attention to how normal people with good memories behave. If you meet someone that impresses you with their ability to remember something, you can ask how they do it. Although be prepared for an "I don't know, I just remember it".

The reality is that to pick up on how people remember, you will need to dig deeper. You may have to ask them what their process is. You may ask what they pay special attention to. But even then, many people do things unconsciously. They don't think about why they are good at something, or bad at something. Be prepared to pay attention to what they pay attention to. Notice what actions they take, and what question they ask. From all this, you can learn new principles of practical memory that you can apply in your life.

Create the Life You Want to Remember

As I've been thinking a lot about memories while writing this book, I realized that we should aim to create the life for ourselves that we would wish to remember. Looking back on key memories is important because it will force you to see what you have done with your life. If you are not happy with what you have accomplished, it is still important to remember, because you can begin to change things to alter the future. If you have lived a life you are unhappy with, and you do not bother to remember it or think about it, then you are likely to continue down the path of making a life you will be unhappy with.

We should not live in denial about our past memories. We should periodically relive them, so we can assess them and improve the memories to come in the future.

Going forward, remember that the actions you take *today* will be your memories of *tomorrow*. Everything that is happening now, is something you will look back on one day. Will you be happy with these memories? If not, take action, and make a positive change.

ISAAC ROBLEDO'S THOUGHTS

I just began a new project to help us all pursue higher states of Consciousness, Understanding, and Being.

If you have enjoyed any of my books, I would be honored if you would read a Thought or two from my new website (I link to it below). These Thoughts involve topics such as:

- The Busy, Entertained, Exhausted Cycle
- The Pursuit of Higher Understanding
- From Feelings of Worthlessness to Worthiness
- Find Your Inner Truth
- Balance, Harmony, Contentment

This is a project of love for me, where all I want to do is spread my best Thoughts into the world, to help you *live your best life*.

You can read all of my Thoughts ***for free*** here: https://www.RobledoThoughts.com/

THANK YOU

Thank you for taking the time to read *Practical Memory*. I hope that you found the information useful. Just remember that a key part of the learning process is putting what you read into practice.

Before you go, I want to invite you to pick up your free copy of *Step Up Your Learning: Free Tools to Learn Almost Anything*. All you have to do is click this link (or type it in your browser):

http://mentalmax.net/EN

Also, if you have any questions, comments, or feedback about this book, you can send me a message and I'll get back to you as soon as possible. Please put the title of the book you are commenting on in the subject line. My email address is:

ic.robledo@mentalmax.net

DID YOU LEARN SOMETHING NEW?

If you found value in this book, please review it on Amazon so I can stay focused on writing more great books. Even a short one or two sentences would be helpful.

>> Support I. C. Robledo by Writing A Review Here <<

MORE BOOKS BY ISAAC ROBLEDO

The Intellectual Toolkit of Geniuses

Master Your Focus

The Smart Habit Guide

No One Ever Taught Me How to Learn

Ready, Set, Change

The Secret Principles of Genius

Idea Hacks

365 Quotes to Live Your Life By

7 Thoughts to Live Your Life By

The Insightful Reader

Question Yourself